The Journey Home

Allen Watson

Book #10 in a Series of Commentaries on
A Course in Miracles®

THE CIRCLE OF ATONEMENT

This is the tenth book in a series, each of which deals with a particular theme from the modern spiritual teaching, *A Course in Miracles®*. The books assume a familiarity with the Course, although they might be of benefit even if you have no acquaintance with the Course. If you would like a complete listing of these books and our other publications, a sample copy of our newsletter, or information about The Circle of Atonement, please contact us at the address below.

The Circle of Atonement

Teaching and Healing Center

P.O. Box 4238, West Sedona, AZ 86340

(928) 282-0790 Fax: (928) 282-0523

E-mail: info@circleofa.com

Website: www.circleofa.com

The ideas presented herein are the personal interpretation and understanding of the author, and are not necessarily endorsed by the copyright holder of *A Course in Miracles*: Foundation for *A Course in Miracles*, 41397 Buecking Dr., Temecula, CA 92590. Portions from *A Course in Miracles* ©1975, *Psychotherapy: Purpose, Process and Practice* ©1996, and *Song of Prayer* ©1996, reprinted by permission of the copyright holder.

All references are given for the Second Edition of the Course, and are listed according to the numbering in the Course, rather than according to page numbers. Each reference begins with a letter, which denotes the particular volume or section of the Course and its extensions (T=Text, W=Workbook for Students, M=Manual for Teachers, C=Clarification of Terms, P=*Psychotherapy*, and S=*Song of Prayer*). After this letter comes a series of numbers, which differs from volume to volume:

T, P, or S-chapter.section.paragraph:sentence; e.g., T-24.VI.2:3-4

W-part (I or II).lesson.paragraph:sentence; e.g., W-pI.182.4:1-2

M or C-section.paragraph:sentence; e.g., C-2.5:2

ISBN 1-886602-20-4

Published by The Circle of Atonement: Teaching and Healing Center
Printed in the United States of America

Cover art by James Francis Yax
Design and layout by Phillips Associates

Acknowledgements

More than ever, I need to acknowledge the contribution Robert Perry has made to this book. The opportunity to work with him, going over every line of this book in detailed discussion, has been more than helpful; it has formed an essential part of the development of the concepts presented here, and has been an ongoing lesson in cooperation. Although I have written the words, in many ways this book should bear Robert's name as co-author. It is a very different book—and a much better one—than it would have been had I written it alone.

The careful proofreading of Susan Perry was essential; she and I may disagree at times on particulars of style, but her input has never been anything but helpful. And usually, right. Tom Dunn contributed several useful suggestions. Thanks, too, to Sandy in the office for her patience as I retreated from other duties when this book fell behind schedule.

Most of all, I want to thank you, the readers, who have encouraged me with your responses to my previous books, and who give me the opportunity to learn by teaching.

CONTENTS

Introduction

The Journey Home attempts to set forth a sequential description of the spiritual journey as seen in *A Course in Miracles*. We will identify the separate stages we pass through on our journey "through fear to love,"[1] and will set them in order as they occur in our experience. The idea is to present a map of sorts that we can look at as we set out on the journey, to give us some idea of our destination, and what we must go through to get there.

The Course has two sections that clearly discuss steps in the journey from beginning to end, and there are other passages that discuss parts of the process. The Course, however, never clearly and succinctly sets down one definitive outline of these stages. Instead there are several outlines, different numbers of steps, and steps in some outlines that are omitted in others. I have attempted to develop an outline that includes most of the various descriptions of stages of development in the Course. I have tried to fit various passages from the Course into this outline.

To me, and I hope to you, it is the actual teaching of the Course that is most important, and not my ideas. Therefore, I want to make it clear that this overall outline *is* my own idea, my understanding gleaned from study of the Course. I have discussed and refined it with the help of Robert Perry, but any errors in either the outline itself, or the placement of Course passages within the outline, are my own. The general concept of a spiritual journey is clear in the Course, and the advice the Course gives about the journey will be relevant whether or not I get the passages in exactly the right order. (Realizing this was a great relief to me in writing this book!)

[1] T-16.IV.11:1

Chapter 1

A Preview of the Map

Before we engage in detailed discussion of the various steps along the journey home to God as seen in *A Course in Miracles,* I want to give you an overall preview of the map. It helps to get the big picture, I think, before we look at the details.

The Course refers to our spiritual journey as "a journey without distance" and says it is simply reawakening to the knowledge of where we always are.[1] There is really nowhere to go because we never left home. However, we believe we left home, and so there is a journey to take, although it occurs entirely within our minds as our false belief in separation from God is gradually undone. Eventually our mind recognizes the fact that we have "arrived" at the place we never left: At home in God.

Therefore, the whole journey we will be looking at is an illusion. The journey is not real, but it seems real to us because we believe we did leave home. We have the illusion of separation, and therefore we need the illusion of a journey that takes us home, in order to dispel the illusion of separation.

As I read the Course, before the journey starts we are in a state of wrong-mindedness, very much identified with our separate ego identity. The journey begins with a turning point, which may be anything from a quiet choice to a major crisis. It continues through a period of split-mindedness consisting of two major phases, becoming progressively easier as it goes on, and it ends with what is referred to in the Course as "the real world," or the state of right-mindedness.

The focus of this book is the first half of the journey. We will also discuss the turning point that begins it, the second half of the journey, and what follows the journey, but since most of us are probably near the beginning, the first half seems to merit more discussion.

The Course uses several different images to represent the beginning and end of our journey, and what lies beyond it: we journey from wrong-mindedness to right-mindedness, but beyond that is One-mindedness; we journey from the world to the real world, which lies at the gate of Heaven, but beyond that is Heaven itself; we travel from false perception to true perception, but beyond perception lies knowledge; we "travel but in dreams"[2] from a nightmare to a happy dream, but beyond the dream lies full awakening.

The journey of which we speak is simply the transition from one state of mind to another, within the dream. For the sake of simplicity, I will use the terms *wrong-mindedness* and *right-mindedness* to identify the starting and ending points of the journey. We could equally well use any of the others terms: the world and the real world; false perception and true perception; or the nightmare and the happy dream.

You may wish to refer to the chart at the end of this chapter for a helpful overview of the journey as you read.

The Starting Point: Wrong-Mindedness

Wrong-mindedness is the state of mind which listens to the ego and makes illusions of separate selves in the world.[3] Wrong-mindedness depends on thoughts of attack and conflict between separate individuals, or between man and God, and therefore requires constant use of judgment. This is the basis of the ego; without it the ego cannot continue. So in simple terms, the "wrong mind" is a mind dominated by the ego thought system and identified with it.

When something occurs to disturb this state of mind and to raise it to question, the turning point has occurred. The journey home begins.

The Turning Point

At some point in our lives something happens that causes us to question our whole mind-set. It can be as simple as an awareness that what we think we know is not all there is to truth, or that there must be

Allen Watson

a better way of handling life. Often, however, some dramatic event is required to shake us loose; a sickness, the death of someone close, the failure of a marriage or a business, a near-death experience, or some kind of powerful spiritual awakening. The Course calls this fundamental change of direction a "turning point."

Everyone is on a spiritual journey whether they realize it or not. When I speak of the journey here, however, I am referring to our *conscious* spiritual journey. Our conscious journey usually begins with some kind of turning point, in which we admit that something in our life is not working, or that nothing is working, and we seek for an answer, a "better way."[4] This may involve deep despair as our hopes of finding happiness in and through the world fail over and over. Once this occurs, and is accepted, at least to some extent, we enter the first phase of the journey.

Phase One: Escaping from Darkness

Phase One of the journey has to do mostly with identifying and escaping from the darkness of our ego thoughts. As we begin we must recognize ourselves as the source of the problem. This first phase is the hardest part of the journey. It involves learning that nothing outside of us is attacking us, and therefore our return attack is not justifiable; that no one is doing it to us, we are doing it to ourselves; that our own choices are causing our experience. It is uncovering the ego, undoing our denial and projection. It usually entails fear and conflict.

Although the Course is full of warnings about the difficulties we almost certainly will encounter, it also is filled with wonderful encouragement to help us through the hardest parts, and we will be looking at both the obstacles and the comforts offered in the Course.

Phase One can be divided into two steps.

Step One: Beginning Thought Reversal

Step One is the very beginning of our thought reversal. It occurs immediately after we have first allowed the idea of a "better way" to take root in our minds. The entry of a new thought, love instead of fear, immediately creates conflict with the old, existing thought system, and this conflict is often fierce.

Step Two: Preferring the New Thoughts

In Step Two, we are applying the new thought increasingly to more and more situations. We accumulate experiences showing us that while the old thoughts always result in fear or pain, the new thoughts bring love and joy. We begin to value the new thought system more than our old thought system, although we still have a divided allegiance.

Phase Two: Emerging into the Light

This phase I have called "emerging into the light" because the balance has shifted and the direction has become clear. Phase Two is initiated when we begin to realize that God's Will is the *only* thing we want, and that His Will is something we must experience together. It is the stage of steady and increasingly determined vigilance *for* God and His Kingdom, and *against* the ego. It is a phase which requires considerable effort on our part, until we reach the end, where effortlessness lies. Yet it is an easier period because the conflict of divided loyalties, characteristic of Phase One, is largely behind us.

Like the first phase, Phase Two can be divided into two steps: an initial period of rest in which we begin to extend our healing to others; and the long road of vigilance and joining together which follows.

Step Three: The Beginnings of Extension

Step Three is an initial period of rest that comes when our mental conflict, which characterized Phase One, comes to an end. We realize that the way out of conflict between opposing thought systems is very simple: choose one wholeheartedly.

During Step Three we begin to gather our holy relationship companions who will journey with us. Identifying completely with the thought system of the Holy Spirit means identifying with the whole Sonship, because He is "the shared Inspiration of all the Sonship."[5] We realize that salvation is not individual but collective. We begin to extend ourselves to the Sonship; as we lead them home, they lead us home.

Step Four: Vigilance for God

Step Four involves what the Course calls "vigilance." When we first enter Phase Two we experience rest because our mental conflict, our divided allegiance, has largely ended. We soon realize, however, that the ego has not been transcended simply because we have made a clear-cut decision for the Kingdom; remnants of its thought system remain buried, undiscovered, within our minds. These remnants must be uncovered and uprooted.

We guard our thoughts against these remnants, choosing more and more consistently against conflict and attack, and for peace, bringing our minds into union with the Holy Spirit, and asking in all circumstances what God's Will is. We relinquish all independent judgment and submit all our thoughts to His judgment.

Our relationships are an effective classroom for learning vigilance. Our companions mirror our projections and help us uncover and release our hidden thoughts.

In Step Four we walk in patience, full of hope, and certain in our knowledge of the final outcome, reinforced by the gifts of peace and joy God continually gives to us.

The Goal of the Journey: The Real World

As was said earlier, the journey's goal is right-mindedness, or the real world. *Right-mindedness* is the state of mind which listens to the Holy Spirit and forgives the world.[6] It is the final vision, "the condition in which God takes the final step Himself."[7] This is the last stopping point before the final step, which is taken by God; therefore, right-mindedness is the goal of the Course for us.

The real world is another term for the same thing. "This is the journey's end. We have referred to it as the real world."[8] The real world is described as

> a borderland where place and time and choice have meaning still, and yet it can be seen that they are temporary, out of place, and every choice has been already made.[9]

In other words, the real world is still a world of form, in time, but one in which place and time are seen as illusions. We still seem to be making meaningful choices, yet we realize we are just living out a choice made long ago, before time began. In the real world, although still *in* the world, we realize that we are, in reality, "at home in God, dreaming of exile."[10]

Perhaps the simplest way to understand the real world is to say that it is the state of mind in which Jesus lived while on earth. In that condition of right-mindedness, he heard no other voice but the Voice for God.[11] The end of the journey to which the Course is leading us is simply that unmixed state of mind.

When we reach the end of the journey, we have not left the world; we have forgiven it completely. Many of us tend to think that the goal of the Course is to get us to Heaven and out of this world. Or, we think the goal is to awaken from our dream of sin and death. Yet the Course makes it abundantly clear, in many, many places, that those are *not* the purpose of the curriculum, although those *are* the ultimate goals. The Course defines its purpose as preparing us for Heaven, not as taking us there.

When you travel by air, your only responsibility is to get yourself to the airport and onto the plane; from there, the pilot will take you the rest of the way. Jesus says repeatedly that "the last step is taken by God."[12] Our journey ends at the real world; God will take us the remaining step, out of the world of perception and into knowledge. It is not a step we can contribute to because, in eternity, it is already complete.

The Last Step:
Beyond the Journey to One-Mindedness

One-mindedness is the state in which the Holy Spirit's Mind exists. He is part of our mind as well as part of God's Mind. One-mindedness is equivalent to the term *knowledge*. In One-mindedness there is no more duality; no subject-object relationship in which perception is necessary. One-mindedness is what lies beyond the point at which the pathway ceases.

The last step and the Oneness that it brings take us far beyond even the glory of the real world to a condition that is literally indescribable.

> Oneness is simply the idea God is. And in His Being, He encompasses all things. No mind holds anything but Him. We say "God is," and then we cease to speak, for in that knowledge words are meaningless. There are no lips to speak them, and no part of mind sufficiently distinct to feel

that it is now aware of something not itself. It has united with its Source. And like its Source Itself, it merely is.

We cannot speak nor write nor even think of this at all. It comes to every mind when total recognition that its will is God's has been completely given and received completely. It returns the mind into the endless present, where the past and future cannot be conceived. It lies beyond salvation; past all thought of time, forgiveness and the holy face of Christ. The Son of God has merely disappeared into his Father, as his Father has in him. The world has never been at all. Eternity remains a constant state.

This is beyond experience we try to hasten.[13]

Note that the Course clearly says that One-mindedness is beyond the experience which is its goal. A state of right-mindedness must precede any transition to One-mindedness. You cannot jump from a wrong-minded state to a One-minded state. You must first move from wrong- to right-mindedness; doing so is the entire purpose of the Course, and the goal of all our efforts. The ultimate goal, the goal beyond the goal, is this Oneness: God Himself. That is the goal of our desire, and the Course often reminds us that God is our eternal goal.

God is our only goal, but in the meantime, while we believe there is a journey, our aim is not to reach that goal but to prepare ourselves for it, to ready our minds for the last step, which God Himself will take.

The Territory of the Journey

The territory covered by our spiritual journey, then, consists of the mental terrain we move through in making our transition from the illusory world to the real world, or from wrong- to right-mindedness. In each picture of the journey, the Course is clear that its task, and ours, ends at the gate of Heaven. When we have been prepared by our journey, God will take us home. He will awaken us to full knowledge, One-mindedness, and perfect Love.

Between wrong-mindedness and right-mindedness is a period in which we experience having a *split* mind. This is the period covered by our journey. Our mind is undivided, never truly split. But in our journey, as we transition between the two states of mind, we vacillate between wrong- and right-mindedness. It seems as if we are in conflict within ourselves; a war begins to rage in our minds. It is this experience of inner conflict that makes the first part of the journey so difficult. The journey becomes easier as we go because, more and more, we transfer our loyalty to the new thought system we are learning from the Holy Spirit. As we make the journey we go back and forth, sometimes identified with the ego, sometimes with the Christ. In the real world, we will become stable in our identification with our true Identity as God's Son.

The oneness of Heaven seems a far-off, distant goal, but it is beyond our concern. We need only be willing to prepare ourselves for that last great transition. When we are ready, God will take the last step for us.

---

[1] T-8.VI.9:6-7
[2] T-13.VII.17:7
[3] C-1.6:1
[4] T-2.III.3:6
[5] T-5.I.7:1
[6] C-1.5:2
[7] C-5.5:3
[8] T-26.III.3:1-2
[9] T-26.III.3:6
[10] T-10.I.2:1
[11] T-5.II.3:9-11
[12] See T-5.I.6:6; T-7.I.6:3; T-11.VIII.15:5; T-13.VIII.3:2; T-17.II.4:5
[13] W-pI.169.5:1-7:1

The Journey

Starting Point	The Turning Point				Goal of the Curriculum	God's Last Step	Ultimate Goal
	Phase One: Escaping from Darkness		Phase Two: Emerging into Light				
	Step One: Beginning Thought Reversal	Step Two: Preferring the New Thoughts	Step Three: Beginnings of Extension	Step Four: Vigilance for God and His Kingdom			
Wrong-mindedness	Conflicting thought systems	Diminishing conflict	Determination to end conflict	Vigilant against conflict	Right-mindedness		One-mindedness
The World	Fear as ego is uncovered	Increasing willingness to see my ego as the problem	Decision to hear only Holy Spirit	Watchfulness for unrecognized ego thoughts	Real World		Heaven
False Perception	Learning I cannot be attacked by anything external	Learning my attacks on others are unjustified	Joining with companions on the journey	Extending forgiveness to my brothers and the world	True Perception		Knowledge
Nightmare					Happy Dream		Awakening

Chapter 2

The Purpose of Knowing the Map

Why study the stages of the spiritual journey anyway? What purpose does it serve to know in advance a general map of the territory we all must move through on the way home to God? Is it really useful in making the journey?

It must have some significance to us because Jesus included quite a bit of information about it in his Course. In *The Song of Prayer*, in one discussion of the journey, he speaks of the ladder of prayer. While making it clear that the journey is an illusion, he also emphasizes that the stages of the journey need to be understood.

> Prayer in its earliest forms is an illusion, because there is no need for a ladder to reach what one has never left. Yet prayer is part of forgiveness as long as forgiveness, itself an illusion, remains unattained. Prayer is tied up with learning until the goal of learning has been reached. And then all things will be transformed together, and returned unblemished into the Mind of God. Being beyond learning, this state cannot be described. *The stages necessary to its attainment, however, need to be understood*, if peace is to be restored to God's Son, who lives now with the illusion of death and the fear of God.[1]

Yet, speaking frankly, I hesitated to write this book because I can envision a lot of ways this kind of information can be misused. So I'd like to point out some ways the concept of stages of spiritual development can be misapplied. After that, I will give some ideas about what I believe makes this information useful to us.

Misuses of the Map

Categorizing and Comparing

I once studied a spiritual teaching that presented seven very clearly defined stages of spiritual development. Followers of the teaching knew these stages and their definitions very well. They had a tendency I found quite distressing; they tried to categorize books, teachers, and each other into one of the stages. You would hear remarks like, "*A Course in Miracles*? Oh, that's only a Fourth Stage book," implying it was less deserving of interest than their "Seventh Stage" teacher. Or you might have someone point out a person across the room and say, in awed tones, "John is a Fifth Stage practitioner." Everybody and everything was classed according to what stage they were in.

Understanding the stages of development in the Course is not meant to provide some means of categorizing and comparing other people and yourself. The map is not intended to enable you to figure out how far you have gone on the journey so as to identify who is ahead of you and who is behind you. Comparison is an ego device that the loving mind does not engage in.[2]

A Source of Discouragement

When you look at the map you automatically try to figure out where you are. It's inevitable that you do this. The map the Course presents, for the most part, can be discouraging in this respect because you are very near the beginning! Take heart, however; you're in pretty good company. Jesus says in the *Psychotherapy* pamphlet, "Most professional therapists are still at the very start of the beginning stage of the first journey."[3] So are we all. In fact, if you are tempted to locate yourself halfway along the map, or nearly home, you are probably wrong. "For you have barely started to allow your first, uncertain steps to be directed up the ladder separation led you down."[4]

The point of the map is to show us how to get from where we think we are, in a faraway land distant from God, back home to God. Of course we are at the start of the map! The information we need is what lies ahead, not what is past. So don't be discouraged by the apparent length of the journey yet ahead of you.

Mistaking the Map for the Territory

Some of us seem to think that if we understand something, we have learned it. Understanding the map does not mean you've made it home; it just means you know the way to get there. Knowing the stages of the journey should not induce lethargy, complacency, or smugness. If I want to go to Vancouver, studying the route from Sedona to Vancouver does not mean I've been to Vancouver. Knowing the route should encourage me in taking the next step, not to sit back and think, "now I know the way," or even, "I am already there."

Making the Journey Real

The main danger of classifying ourselves or one another as being in a certain part of the journey is not that we are likely to be inaccurate—which is certainly true. The worst danger is that we come to *equate* a person with a certain level of development. "She is just beginning so she can't practice vigilance yet," or, "He is so far advanced he can't possibly need to be reminded not to pursue some earthly goal for happiness." We are not supposed to see people as in Step One or Step Three; we are supposed to see *everyone* as already finished with the journey, "as if he had already gone far beyond his actual accomplishments in time."[5]

The Course warns often against making error real. Categorizing is just one way of making the *journey* real, as if the person's stage of development within time were more important, or more real, than their eternal perfection.

Benefits of Knowing the Map

You Can't Start Until You Know Where You're Going

The only way to get to a goal is to head in its direction, not away from it.[6] The Course repeatedly restates its goal for its students. It is vital to understand what the goal of the Course is if you want to achieve it; that should be common sense. Likewise, it can be equally useful to know what the goal *is not*, or you might waste a lot of time trying to reach an unrealistic goal.

Knowing the Expected Pitfalls

When you set out on a long automobile trip it can be very helpful to call the Auto Club and get information about detours, road construction, and so on. In describing the steps of the journey, the Course lets us know about several pitfalls we may encounter on the way. Knowing in advance that long-hidden fears may surface when you begin to practice the Course, for instance, can be very helpful; otherwise, when the fear arises you may be tempted to panic and abandon the Course.

When we know the pitfalls along the way we will pay attention to the instructions concerning what to do when we encounter them. When we encounter rough pavement, so to speak, we won't be surprised or think we've lost the way. We'll simply slow down or take the recommended detour.

Not Getting Ahead of Yourself

Some parts of the Course describe the end of the journey, and that can be so attractive we may feel we want to be there *now*. I may be in Sedona reading a description of the scenery in Vancouver and think, "Wow! I really want to get there." But to get there I have to go through (or fly over) a lot of other territory. I can't just teleport from Arizona to British Columbia without passing through the territory in between. And if I know that a town is on the route, and I have not yet passed it, I can know that I'm not in Vancouver yet.

Likewise, in following the Course, we cannot skip stages. Another benefit of the map is alerting us to *what comes first* and *what comes next* in the spiritual journey. There is no sense in vainly striving to attain the real world if we haven't bothered with the steps in between. You can't just leap from total egoity into the real world; there is a natural process of development. A map of the spiritual journey can help to keep us realistic about our spiritual progress and to focus on things appropriate to our level of development. The map can help us be patient, instead of crying, "Daddy, are we there yet?"

The Map as Hologram

The map of the journey can help us on a short-term basis as well as long-term. If we look at the two basic phases of the journey given in Chapter One, they can be seen as describing either of two different things. First, they can be seen to describe the stages of experience within a particular occasion of forgiveness, which may occupy only a short moment of time. Second, they can describe the general, overall stages we pass through in the spiritual journey, which takes a lifetime, or perhaps many lifetimes.

I believe that the stages presented in the Course can be understood in both ways. The spiritual process can be thought of as holographic, in that every individual experience of salvation contains all the stages, from beginning to end, and yet, overall, the progress of our spiritual development will pass through these same stages during our long return home. The stages describe both the entire journey and points within the journey. The Course itself seems to be saying that every moment of our lives is, in a certain sense, a recapitulation of the entire fall from grace:

> Each day, and every minute in each day, and every instant that each minute holds, you but relive the single instant when the time of terror took the place of love.[7]

Another passage then graphically describes the decision facing us in every moment:

> Each day, each hour and minute, even each second, you are deciding between the crucifixion and the resurrection; between the ego and the Holy Spirit.[8]

As I understand it every instant of salvation is complete. Every instant contains the whole. A flash of forgiving insight *is* the real world, intruding for just a moment into our dark dream. To attain that instant of relief, we must pass through all the stages of spiritual development *in that instant*. In terms of the two phases of the journey, we recognize our responsibility, realize "I am doing this," and then join with the Holy Spirit in seeing our error as illusion, letting it go, and making a choice for God's Kingdom.

At the same time, over the course of our lives, we begin with a primary emphasis on the first of those two steps, which is withdrawing blame from things outside of us, and taking the responsibility for our lives back within to the mind, where it belongs. You might call this first stage the *negative* stage, because it consists of unmasking our illusions, and often involves fear. Over time, as we accept the first lesson, we spend more and more of our moments in holy instants, joined with the Holy Spirit, choosing with Him and against the ego. This might be called the *positive* stage because it involves realizing our innocence as well as the innocence of others. So the stages apply both to particular, short-term experiences of salvation, and to the longer term experience of *development* in salvation.

We do not go through this process of recognizing that the guilt outside is really inside, and then letting it go, just one time in our lives. We go through the process thousands of times. We start with experiencing it in a specific situation, and experience it again and again in similar situations, until we have learned to recognize that particular type of situation, and to avoid our projection of guilt in that area. But there are hundreds of such areas in our lives. Our progress through the stages over the long-term comes as we increasingly learn to generalize, and to recognize the same identical patterns in what appear to be dissimilar situations. When we have applied the lesson universally to everything and everyone in our lives, we will have attained the real world.

When we see the phases of the journey in this holographic way, trying to categorize people into spiritual boxes becomes much more difficult. Since categorizing and comparing is something we should avoid, that is a beneficial result. A person may have advanced spiritually so that he is living, most of the time, in Phase Two. And yet at any given moment, with any given circumstance, his greatest need may be a Phase One recognition: a letting go of blaming something outside his mind for what he is experiencing. Conversely, a person may be at the very beginning of the path and yet experience a clear and unequivocal episode of the highest spiritual realization. Thus, in a certain sense, seen from the larger perspective, we all pass through these steps from beginning to end during our spiritual journey, although we can all be in any of the steps at any given instant.

---

[1] S-1.II.8:3-8, my italics
[2] T-24.II.1:1
[3] P-3.II.8:5
[4] T-28.III.1:2
[5] T-2.V.10:1
[6] T-31.IV.7:3
[7] T-26.V.13:1
[8] T-14.III.4:1

Chapter 3

The Journey Begins

The Holy Spirit, Our Guarantee of Safe Arrival

How could a mind totally identified with the ego's thoughts of sin, guilt, fear, scarcity, attack, and counter-attack ever break free to find its way home? How could it even begin? If that were an accurate description of our minds, they could not break free. The mind could not begin because it would not even suspect that a journey existed. Ego is totally out of touch with spirit; "Nothing can reach spirit from the ego, and nothing can reach the ego from spirit."[1] But God did not allow our awareness of home to be obliterated by the ego. He gave us the Holy Spirit.

The story of separation we have taught ourselves is a tragic tale. It is the story of how we all got here, according to our belief. We seem to be a bunch of individual beings living in bodies in a physical world, with no visible contact with God. What we experience as our selves is only a tiny, fenced-off portion of what we really are. We are all fragmented aspects of one mind, deluded into thinking we are separate individuals. Every person in our lives is really a part of our one Self.

These individual aspects of one mind, believing they are separate beings, have projected themselves into the physical world in bodies that "embody" the ego concept. We chose to come here because we thought it was a place God could not enter; we came to hide from Him. We chose to come here to suffer the death we thought we deserved. We wrote the soap opera script of our lives and came to act it out, and we made up the other characters we wanted to interact with, just as we do in our dreams. We have invented the world we see.

Since creation there has been something in us that is irresistibly drawn to God. Love is always attracted to love, and since God created us as love, love is still what we are. Despite our best efforts to escape God and forget our Self, we cannot escape the power of this internal compulsion. It is our nature. It is our destiny. That is why we must all inevitably find home—we cannot escape our Self.

Our thoughts of separation did cast a shroud over our Self, but could not change it in any way. We did not succeed in escaping from God. He planted a seed in our mind that must bear fruit: the Holy Spirit. The instant we had the thought of separation, God sent His Holy Spirit into our darkened minds as the Answer to separation. "The instant the idea of separation entered the mind of God's Son, in that same instant was God's Answer given."[2] Our right mind, the Christ Mind, remains as it always was, and in it lives the Holy Spirit.

> The Holy Spirit abides in the part of your mind that is part of the Christ Mind. He represents your Self and your Creator, Who are One. He speaks for God and also for you, being joined with Both.[3]

God's Word is given every mind which thinks that it has separate thoughts, and will replace these thoughts of conflict with the Thought of peace.

> The Thought of peace was given to God's Son the instant that his mind had thought of war....when the mind is split there is a need of healing. So the Thought that has the power to heal the split became a part of every fragment of the mind that still was one, but failed to recognize its oneness.[4]

Only because of these things—our unchanged Self and the Holy Spirit—are we even able to begin this journey. We have not been able to entirely block the light of God from our minds. There is still in every one of us some faint glimmer of that light, a spark, so that we can remember. We can find our way home. We not only can; every one of us *will* find our way.

Several passages in the Text speak of this internal preparation for the journey that has been given to every one of us. We are told:

- Every living thing shares a universal Will to be whole.[5]
- We all have a spark of light in us, a call of creation to guide us home.[6]

Allen Watson

- The Holy Spirit is in us as an Eternal Guest; our choice to think like Him fans the spark into a flame.[7]
- By turning to the light, the spark can sweep us out of all darkness.[8]

So the journey is already begun, because we all have that spark within us. *Everyone* is on a spiritual journey; it is just that most of us have not realized it. We have a head start, an irresistible drawing to God, and a Guide to show us the way. And because of that eternal spark, "Ultimately, every member of the family of God must return."[9]

> Everyone here has entered darkness, yet no one has entered it alone. Nor need he stay more than an instant. For he has come with Heaven's Help within him, ready to lead him out of darkness into light at any time. The time he chooses can be any time, for help is there, awaiting but his choice.[10]

The Start of the Journey

Our conscious spiritual journey begins when, at some point in our lives, we encounter something that prompts a change in direction. We make a choice for that new direction, which brings a new thought, something contrary to the ego thought system, into our minds.

Recognizing Our Misery

Towards the beginning of Chapter 8 of the Text, we are told that the very first change that is introduced is a change in direction:

> The curriculum of the Atonement is the opposite of the curriculum you have established for yourself [the ego curriculum], but so is its outcome. If the outcome of yours has made you unhappy, and if you want a different one, a change in the curriculum is obviously necessary. The first change to be introduced is a change in direction.[11]

Basically, this is how the journey begins for many, if not most, of us: We recognize that the way we have been conducting our lives is not making us happy. We recognize our wrong-mindedness. It may take us a long, long time to come to this point. As the *est* seminars used to say, we are like rats programmed to find food in a maze; we keep going down the same tunnel long after the food is gone. We obstinately insist that we know the way to happiness and keep pursuing it, even after hundreds of failures.

> Seek not outside yourself. For all your pain comes simply from a futile search for what you want, insisting where it must be found. What if it is not there? Do you prefer that you be right or happy?[12]

It can take us a long while to come to the "astounding" realization that being happy is better than being right. It is so very hard for us to admit that we are wrong.

Sometimes this turning point can be reached in what might be called a positive way rather than a negative way: a peak spiritual experience which shows us, by contrast, the emptiness of life as we have been living it. Everyone must come to the point of realizing the world as we know it is without value—indeed, that "there is no world"[13]—but the lesson comes in different forms to different people, in ways "which they can understand and recognize."[14] Not everyone bottoms out in despair; some see a vision of another world that launches them on their path.

> Some see it suddenly on point of death, and rise to teach it. Others find it in experience that is not of this world, which shows them that the world does not exist because what they behold must be the truth, and yet it clearly contradicts the world.
>
> And some will find it in this course, and in the exercises that we do today.[15]

Sometimes the beginning of the spiritual journey looks like—and *feels* like—the road to hell. We have to recognize our misery before we can desire to change it. We have thrown away our birthright to joy, and don't realize we've done it.

> How can you teach someone the value of something he has deliberately thrown away? He must have thrown it away because he did not value it. You can only show him how miserable he is without it, and slowly bring it nearer so he can learn how his misery lessens as he approaches it.[16]

That is a very good description of the beginning of our journey, and the first steps along the way. Once we realize we are miserable, we turn in another direction. The Holy Spirit then slowly brings us nearer to our union with Him, gently showing us how our misery diminishes as we follow His lead.

> You who are steadfastly devoted to misery must first recognize that you are miserable and not happy. The Holy Spirit cannot teach without this contrast, for you believe that misery *is* happiness.[17]

The journey begins with a realization of unhappiness. It may be an extreme experience of misery and despair if nothing less will induce us to change our direction. We have to recognize the *cost* of our mistakes before we are willing to give them up.

The Turning Point

"The journey of a thousand miles begins with a single step." So says an ancient Chinese proverb. So it is with our spiritual journey. "Think like Him ever so slightly, and the little spark becomes a blazing light that fills your mind."[18] It begins in crisis or perhaps inauspiciously, as we simply make a turn in the right direction.

With many of us the turning point is not terribly dramatic. We may not even be able to identify the moment as we look back. It can be as simple as it was with Helen Schucman and Bill Thetford: a simple statement made by Bill, "There must be another way," and Helen's agreement to help him find that way. All it takes to begin the journey is to end our struggle against the drawing power of love, just for a second. All it takes is just once to raise to question the judgments of our ego, and think, "Is this the only way to see things?" The beginning of the journey is just a moment of willingness to see things differently, a moment of doubting the ego, a moment of despair in which we cry out to God for an answer, a moment in which we see the interests of another to be identical with our own. Most of us who have begun to study the Course have had such a moment; most of us have begun.

The passage that most succinctly describes the various steps of the journey comes early in the Text.[19] You may wish to read the entire two paragraphs together, now. The section describes the turning point like this:

The acceptance of the Atonement by everyone is only a matter of time....An imprisoned will engenders a situation which, in the extreme, becomes altogether intolerable. Tolerance for pain may be high, but it is not without limit. Eventually everyone begins to recognize, however dimly, that there *must* be a better way. As this recognition becomes more firmly established, it becomes a turning point.[20]

The journey home often begins with a situation that becomes intolerably painful, until we finally are willing to look for "a better way" (a reference to the famous incident between Helen Schucman and Bill Thetford which gave birth to the Course). Pain and despair drive us to be willing to change our direction, and as the recognition that there must be another way becomes firm, we reach the turning point. The journey begins.

Whether we reach the turning point dramatically or in some more commonplace way, we all must eventually reach the point of losing hope in this world so that we can go beyond it.

And learning they [the roads of this world] led nowhere, lost their hope. And yet this was the time they could have learned their greatest lesson. All must reach this point, and go beyond it.[21]

If we still think the answer is within the world's framework, what reason would we have to look beyond it? Why would we ever say, "There must be another way?" The journey must begin with a turn in the right direction. Learning "there is no hope of answer in the world"[22] is needful, but not enough. Alone, that realization can lead to suicide. We must go beyond it, to the realization that a better way must exist, and the determination to find it.

One New Thought Changes Everything

Once we are willing to consider "another way," the Holy Spirit introduces some new idea into our minds. He does not need to flood us with new thoughts; one is enough. "One thought, completely unified, will serve to unify all thought."[23] He uses the idea, for instance, that "to give and to receive are one in truth."[24]

To learn that giving and receiving are the same has special usefulness, because it can be tried so easily and seen as true. And when this special case has proved it always works, in every circumstance when it is tried, the thought behind it can be generalized to other areas of doubt and double vision. And from there it will extend, and finally arrive at the one Thought which underlies them all.[25]

The single idea that giving and receiving are the same, introduced into the mind, will eventually totally sabotage the ego thought system. The ego's thought system, like the Holy Spirit's, is totally consistent. This foreign thought does not fit the system. Eventually, if the thought is not rejected, it causes the entire thought system of the ego to be re-evaluated and discarded.

Any thought of truth will do; it does not have to be the "giving is receiving" thought. That thought just happens to work particularly well because, as Jesus says, it is so easily tried and proven to be true. Any true idea, any part of the Holy Spirit's thought system, when injected into our mind, will work. It could be, "I am never upset for the reason I think."[26] It could be, "God's Son is innocent."[27] It could be, "I am doing this to myself."[28] The ego thought system is a house of cards; pull out any card and the entire structure will eventually crumble. This can be through introducing a new thought, or perhaps a new experience that contradicts the ego's thoughts.

> One vision, clearly seen, that does not fit the picture as it was perceived before will change the world for eyes that learn to see, because the concept of the self has changed.[29]

Have one experience of forgiveness and you have experienced yourself as a forgiving, loving being. That does not fit the ego's picture of you. A moment of joining with another person, seeing them as a friend instead of enemy, can change your world.

Ever Deeper Beginnings

We have all already begun the journey, for it began when God lit the lamp in our minds and planted the Holy Spirit there to remind us of the light. We began again, more consciously, at some turning point in our lives in which we questioned our ego's judgment. Perhaps, in despair, we said, "There must be another way," and began to look for it. We experienced a change in direction, and some thought contrary to the ego system entered our mind and found a tentative home there.

We began, yet in all likelihood we all will experience this "beginning" phase again, more than once. Like all the stages of the journey, this one is holographic, and our experience of it does not diminish; it grows. Every turn away from the ego starts with a recognition of the cost of listening to the ego, the misery of heart we feel when we listen to its voice, and the fervent desire for a better way. That recognition does not peak out at the beginning; it stays with us until the end.

The stages of the journey are cumulative. Each successive stage includes all that come before it, and so this "beginning" of the journey may be a lesson we learn and relearn, over and over, for the rest of our lives.

---

[1] T-4.I.2:6
[2] M-2.2:6
[3] C-6.4:1-3
[4] W-pII.2.2:1, 3-4
[5] T-31.I.9:1
[6] T-10.IV.7:5-8:2; 8:6-7
[7] T-11.II.5:2,4
[8] T-11.III.5:6
[9] T-1.V.4:1
[10] T-25.III.6:1-4
[11] T-8.I.5:1-3
[12] T-29.VII.1:6-9
[13] W-pI.132.6:2 and 7:1
[14] W-pI.132.7:2
[15] W-pI.132.7:3-8:1
[16] T-4.VI.5:1-3
[17] T-14.II.1:2-3
[18] T-11.II.5:4
[19] T-2.III.3-4
[20] T-2.III.3:1, 4-7
[21] T-31.IV.3:5-7
[22] T-31.IV.4:3
[23] W-pI.108.5:1
[24] W-pI.108.Heading
[25] W-pI.108.6:1-3
[26] W-pI.5.Heading
[27] T-31.I.7:11
[28] Based on T-27.VIII.10:1
[29] T-31.VI.5:4

Chapter 4

Escaping from Darkness: Phase One, Step One

When we allowed the Holy Spirit to inject His thought into our awareness, a pocket of right-mindedness formed in our minds that will expand until it engulfs the whole mind. That final outcome is certain. How long it will take depends only on our willingness to cooperate.

The journey home is not what we expect it to be. After a turning point in which we open ourselves to God, weakly or strongly, we expect things to get progressively better. Instead, very often, they seem to get worse. Many people, if they are not prepared for this, begin to suspect that their turn towards spirit was a big mistake, or that they are going about it all wrong.

We need to take a careful look at the first part of the journey, then, to see what some of its distressing symptoms are, why they occur, how we often react to these symptoms, and what the Course recommends we do about them.

Phase One: Course Culture Shock

Most people who visit a foreign country for an extended time experience something called "culture shock." The Random House Dictionary defines the phrase as meaning, "a state of bewilderment and distress experienced by an individual who is suddenly exposed to a new, strange, or foreign social and cultural environment." Phase One of the journey is Course culture shock, the ultimate experience of an encounter with a system of thought and perception that is the complete opposite of everything our ego has taught us.

The turning point introduced the idea of another way of seeing the world. This better way is rooted in the realization that our problems are caused, not by things outside us, but by the way we have been looking at them. In short, the problem is within us, not outside. We had believed that the ego's perception was the only way to see things. Now we realize there is an alternative, and we are considering that alternative.

There are two general aspects, then, to the shift we have experienced. The first we might call *reversal of projection*. The second could be labeled *opening to an alternative perception*. These two aspects each evoke different symptoms that characterize the earliest steps of our journey.

Reversal of Projection

Before the turning point you practiced projection without a thought about it. The unhappiness and unrest you felt within were projected outside and blamed on the world. You were the victim of the world you saw, and you justified your anger at the world by pointing out what it had done to you. You spent your energy in trying to manipulate and manhandle the world into a shape that would make you happy—an impossible task.

Now you realize that you may have been wrong. Perhaps the problem is not outside, but inside. Perhaps you are the cause of your own suffering. Perhaps what you are seeing in the world is only a reflection of thoughts within your own mind. Therefore, the path to healing lies within, in your own mind, rather than in outward change. Instead of trying to change the world, you will now begin to change your mind about the world.

Symptoms Resulting from Withdrawal of Projection

When you were projecting guilt without questioning yourself about it, you were able to maintain a comfortable, seemingly innocent self-image. Even though your life may not have been a shining example of purity, most of the time you were able to convince yourself that you were a decent, fair-minded, and fundamentally good person. Sure, you had your hang-ups; who doesn't? Nobody's perfect. But despite these "trivial" flaws, you saw yourself as on the side of the angels. Even if you acted out particularly vicious attacks on people in your world, you had good reason for them. You had been severely provoked and mistreated. You were an innocent victim, forced sometimes to react in anger, but in no way responsible for it.

Now, your cover has been blown. You are beginning to see, no doubt with a great deal of reluctance, just how rotten you seem to be. If your anger, for instance, was not caused by that other person, who is left? You. You look at all your screwed up relationships and realize that the common factor in them all is you.

Projection is the outermost defense of the ego, and when it gets removed, the miserable picture of yourself you've been hiding gets uncovered. You feel like the bad person you always feared you were.

This barrage of blame is not what you expected when you opened your heart to God, not by a long shot. It can lead to some particularly unfortunate responses if you do not understand it properly.

Opening to an Alternative Perception

Before the turning point you were devoted to the ego's system of thought, whether you knew it or not. Now you have allowed an alternative into your mind, an alternative that completely contradicts the ego. Inevitably, this produces severe sensations of conflict.

The human mind has an intrinsic need for unity. You can't live comfortably with internal conflict. "Inner peace" is nearly synonymous with a lack of conflicting thoughts. And yet, by the very nature of the choice you have made to consider an alternative, you have introduced conflict into your mind. This conflict may start small but it quickly flares up to monumental proportions, and only gradually diminishes as you pass through the first half of your journey.

Symptoms of the Conflict

The conflict takes on many forms referred to in the Course, some of which may seem familiar to you:

- *disorientation*: feeling no clear frame of reference
- *aimlessness*: no clear sense of purpose or direction
- *confusion*: doubt, lack of any certainty
- *meaninglessness*: old meanings no longer apply and we are uncertain what new meaning there might be
- *instability*: no firm foundation; everything is shifting like the ground in an earthquake

- *ambiguity*: being up in the air
- *futility*: no clear sense of achievement; feeling that you and your life are a big joke
- *depression*: feeling that you can never make it to the end of the journey
- *crisis of identity*: not knowing who you are

All of these things hit you near the start of the journey, according to the Course. It's enough to scare you off, isn't it? That often happens. The early steps of the journey are a crucial time because of these difficulties, and you need help to get through them. The time of conflict is unavoidable, however; with the ego thought system firmly in place there is no way to escape the drastic disagreement introduced by the Holy Spirit. Phase One, in large measure, consists of getting past this conflict.

Conflict and Self-Blame Together

If we combine the self-blame stemming from reversal of projection with internal conflict and confusion, we get an even clearer picture of what is happening within our minds. Prior to the turning point your mind was devoted to the ego thought system, a thought system of hate, attack, guilt, and fear. You concealed that ugly devotion, however; you hid it from the world and from yourself with a mask of innocence. You justified your anger and attack by perceiving guilt in others. You projected the ugliness you did not want to see in yourself onto the world; what you did not want within, you saw without.

Now you have made a tentative choice for the thought system of the Holy Spirit instead of the ego. And you have begun to realize that the darkness you thought was in the world is in your own mind. Your whole mental picture of reality has been turned upside-down! You begin your journey, therefore, in great internal conflict, disorientation, and self-blame.

Symptoms of Conflict and Self-Blame

Confronted with this internal storm you naturally want to escape it. The ego, frantic to survive, quickly points out that "things were better before." It urges you to dump this disruptive new thought system and go back to the way you were before. Partying and getting drunk—if that was your form of escape—may not have held much promise of eternal satisfaction, but at least it was fun *sometimes*. This constant inner conflict is really a drag by comparison.

You may try going back to the old ways. Eventually this proves to be impossible, because you can't quite get rid of the taste of "something else" you found in that turning point. So the ego bounces back in the spirit of, "If you can't beat 'em, join 'em." It attempts to infiltrate your spiritual path and distort it.

Instead of facing the conflict and dealing with it in a straightforward way, by resolving it, the ego characteristically tries to obscure or mute the conflict. It tries to make your path into an ego trip, perhaps convincing you that you can use this new stuff to get really rich or famous or powerful, or perhaps deluding you into feeling superior to the rest of unenlightened humanity.

Or the ego turns your path into a "spiritual" version of projection. You blame your inner conflict, not on your own divided allegiance, but on God, or the world. "God does not answer my prayers." "I could be so spiritual if only the world would support spiritual seekers, if only I didn't have to waste all my time making a living, etc." "I would be much more advanced if only my husband/wife/friends were on the path with me."

There are dozens of ways in which the ego tries to take over our spiritual journey. All of them are really attempts to go backwards and to avoid a final commitment to the new system of thought. All such attempts only prolong the pain rather than relieving it. The Course pleads with us to avoid unnecessary pain:

> Seek not outside yourself. For all your pain comes simply
> from a futile search for what you want, insisting where it
> must be found.[1]

The Recommended Response

Instead of masking the conflict, the response recommended by the Course is to rip off the band-aid. Look the conflict full in the face. Be with it. See it in stark clarity. Realize completely just how opposite to one another ego and spirit really are. Don't hide the conflict, and don't run from it. Face it.

> Conflict must be resolved. It cannot be evaded, set
> aside, denied, disguised, seen somewhere else, called by

another name, or hidden by deceit of any kind, if it would be escaped. It must be seen exactly as it is, where it is thought to be, in the reality which has been given it, and with the purpose that the mind accorded it. For only then are its defenses lifted, and the truth can shine upon it as it disappears.[2]

When you do this, the Course instructs, the blank insanity of the ego becomes evident. Then, because our fundamental nature is one of sanity, we will move in the only direction that can resolve the conflict: we will make a clear-cut choice for God.

The First Two Steps

"The Lessons of the Holy Spirit" (Section V of Chapter 6) is one of the two most complete presentations of the whole journey in the Course.[3] I am going to use this as a framework during our description of the journey, bringing in parallel passages from several other sections of the Course (see footnote 1) as we go along.

The Introduction to Chapter 6 presents three premises of the ego: "I am being attacked; attack in return is justified; and I am in no way responsible for my counter-attack." The reply of the Holy Spirit to each of these premises is its direct opposite: "You cannot *be* attacked, attack *has* no justification, and you *are* responsible for what you believe."[4] The first two steps in the journey, in Phase One, center on our learning the first two lessons. The final phase of the journey is characterized by the lesson concerning responsibility for our thought.

Step One: Beginning of Thought Reversal

As we pass the turning point, we have only just begun. A new thought—giving rather than getting—has entered. We see that an alternative exists, but we are, as yet, by no means convinced of that alternative. What, then, are some of the things we need to know about our first steps in the journey home? This is what we'll be looking at in the rest of this chapter.

A Very Preliminary Step

Step One is "very preliminary."[5] What does "preliminary" mean? According to my dictionary it means "prior to or preparing for the main matter, action, or business." In other words, this step is just our *preparation* for the main journey out of darkness. This is like packing your bags before leaving for the airport; just the preliminary step. Jesus says it is *very* preliminary, so maybe a better analogy would be making up a list of what to pack! Steps One and Two are *both* called preliminary; in a very real sense they are both just leading up to Phase Two, in which we begin to travel in earnest.

The preliminary step is portrayed in "The Lessons of the Holy Spirit" as opening our minds to this lesson: "To have, give all to all." [6] This simple-seeming lesson is going to take us all the way because it contains the seeds of the destruction of the ego's thought system.

Yet how do we stack up to this "very preliminary step"? At best most have only begun to take this idea seriously. I referred earlier to the statement, "For you have barely started to allow your first, uncertain steps to be directed up the ladder separation led you down."[7] Most of us, I think, are still in the early stages of learning this "very preliminary" lesson.

The temptation is to see ourselves as more advanced than we are, to refuse the "beginner's mind" status, as some teachers of Zen call it. This is one way the ego tries to take over the spiritual journey. We may feel that God has chosen us in some special way and has given us an important purpose in the world. While that is true in a certain sense, it is no more true of one person than of another. "All my brothers are special."[8] Self-importance does not mix with our true spiritual function.

We may feel as though we have made a huge leap—and we have. It is important, however, to cultivate our "beginner's mind" and to realize that there is much for us to learn. Shunryu Suzuki, the respected Zen teacher, called "beginner's mind" the "Zen mind." In other words, the most mature state of mind is one that always remains open and teachable, devoid of self-inflation.

Unlearning the Getting Concept

The first lesson of the Holy Spirit presented in the Text, Chapter 6, is, "To have, give all to all," or as it is rephrased later, "*Having* rests on giving, and not on getting."⁹ Giving and receiving are one and the same thing; what we give, we receive; what we give, we recognize as something we have.

Workbook Lesson 108 instructs you to offer everyone who comes to mind things like peace of mind, quietness, and gentleness, and then to notice afterward that the things you offered "come to you in the amount in which" you gave them.¹⁰ In other words, you receive what you gave.

The lesson of giving is also particularly good at breaking us free from identification with the body and the material world. It teaches us that it is possible to give things and receive them, or have them increase, at the same time. As this lesson is absorbed it will gently undermine the entire ego thought system that is based on separation and "getting," which is really a polite way of saying "attack." "To have, give" will provide a new frame of reference that will eventually reconcile all opposites in our mind.

As the Holy Spirit begins to teach us this lesson, the ego will try to convince us that we are being called to sacrifice. We may get angry at God and perceive Him as taking things from us. Ugly feelings of possessiveness may arise. As always, the answer is to face the conflict squarely. Do not deny your unwillingness to give, or that you feel anger at God, if you do. I've found that the best thing to do is to tell Him just how irritated I am. It's remarkable how often, in talking to Him, the foolishness of the anger becomes apparent, and the anger evaporates.

We Only Need Turn

"It is not even necessary that you complete the step yourself, but it is necessary that you turn in that direction."¹¹ What a relief to hear that we don't have to do the whole thing by ourselves! All we need to do is make a turn in the right direction; just open the door a crack and let the idea in: "Maybe the way to have is to give. Maybe what I give is what I receive."

The first step begins with a change of direction, just a little opening to the light. This change of direction is entirely up to us; of all three steps in Chapter 6, this is "the only one you must take for yourself."¹² Until we turn, until we crack open the door, even God Himself will not force His Will upon us. He wants only our willing cooperation. Once we crack open the door, however, the whole power of God floods in to help us. From that instant we are never alone again.

Learning that we are not alone, that Help is with us, is an extremely important part of this first step.

New Difficulties, Especially in Relationships

Although this is a very preliminary step, it is also the most difficult and "hardest lesson to learn."[13] It is hard because our motives are still conflicted, and those around us seem to be witnesses *against* the new idea that has been introduced.

Nearly every initial turning point involves a relationship in some way. In withdrawing projection we are withdrawing it *from someone*. Learning to give rather than get involves relationships. Forgiveness involves others, and so does joining together in a common purpose. Many times in our turning point, a holy relationship has been born, although we may not be aware of it.

When the turning point involves the start of a holy relationship, as it did with Helen Schucman and Bill Thetford, there is a sudden change in the purpose of the relationship from sin to holiness. Instead of serving our private need to get something from the other person, the relationship now has a purpose of helping one another to enjoy wholeness. Before, the relationship was in the form of a bargain, a give and take. Now, the relationship has been turned upside down, and the old form does not fit the new goal. These conflicts that arise in the relationship are just reflections of the inner conflict between thought systems that we discussed earlier.

The change in goal immediately introduces a period of difficulty and discomfort, particularly at the very beginning.

> The period of discomfort that follows the sudden change in a relationship from sin to holiness...[14]

> The only difficult phase is the beginning. For here, the goal of the relationship is abruptly shifted to the exact opposite of what it was.[15]

> At once His goal replaces yours. This is accomplished very rapidly, but it makes the relationship seem disturbed, disjunctive and even quite distressing.[16]

Conscious of mixed motives in ourselves, we remain suspicious of our partner in the relationship because we project our mixed motives onto the partner. Learning to let go of the perception of attack can seem, at times, almost impossible. Perceiving attack in our own minds, we cannot believe that attack is not in the minds of those around us.

The strain on relationships can be so great that "many relationships have been broken off at this point, and the pursuit of the old goal is re-established in another relationship."[17] The temptation in these initial times of difficulty is to abandon the step we have taken and to try to regress. Our ego will tempt us to project our inner conflict onto our relationship partner, blaming her or him for our failure to find inner peace. We think that it will be easier with someone else, someone more compatible. Seldom, if ever, is that the case. What we often are doing is finding a new partner with whom to pursue the old goal, not the new one. While the Holy Spirit often guides people to leave particularly destructive or hopeless relationships, I think that relationship break-ups in general are far more frequently ego-motivated than we would like to believe. In this first blush of new spirituality we need to be careful of looking down on those "less spiritual" than we are, particularly if we are close to them.

You might think it would be better somehow to make the start of the journey easier. After all, if you hit the worst stretch of road just as you start out, you might change your mind and turn back, not realizing that it gets better further on. But Jesus says quite clearly that the initial difficulty is not only very common, it is necessary:

> It would not be kinder to shift the goal more slowly, for the contrast would be obscured, and the ego given time to reinterpret each slow step according to its liking. Only a radical shift in purpose could induce a complete change of mind about what the whole relationship is for. As this change develops and is finally accomplished, it grows increasingly beneficent and joyous. But at the beginning, the situation is experienced as very precarious.[18]

As we begin our journey home, the seeming difficulty can appear almost overwhelming at times. The conflict and difficulty needs to be strong at the start; the contrast must be sharp enough to induce the desire for a complete change of mind. Anything less would fail to

Allen Watson

break through the layers of deception our ego has spread over our minds.

The conflict may seem too much, and we will be tempted to give up before we really begin. Yet Jesus tells us to *be comforted* by the fact that the difficult part is in the beginning.[19] In other words, it gets easier as we go along, and "grows increasingly beneficent and joyous."

There is a hiking trail near Sedona that I have recommended to several friends. The head of the trail is very hard to find, and almost immediately the hiker comes to a washed-out bridge and is forced to ford a stream on slippery rocks. Yet, once on the other side, the path levels out and becomes easy. The spiritual journey is a lot like that. If you expect difficulties at the start, but know that the difficulties do not last forever, it makes going through the difficult period easier.

Things Being Taken Away

In "Development of Trust"[20] the same element of difficulty appears in the first two periods discussed by that section. The first period, "a period of undoing," seems to overlap both what I have called "the turning point" and Step One. The Manual speaks of the journey in terms of learning to give up "the shabby offerings of the ego" in favor of "the gifts of God."[21] The first period, which induces us to make this shift, is one in which "it seems as if things are being taken away."[22] There may be some drastic change in circumstances, such as the breakup of a relationship, loss of a job, or a sudden illness, which forces us to "see things in a different light."[23] Such an event may be our turning point.

Yet the effects of such a turning point rarely disappear overnight. We may be slogging through the aftermath for months or even years as we begin our spiritual journey. Often it is not obvious that we have gained anything at all; we focus on the apparent loss. Any sudden change could be our turning point, and yet not all changes are turning points because we cannot even begin to see them as helpful.

> These changes are always helpful. When the teacher of God has learned that much, he goes on to the next stage.[24]

This sort of turning point is usually experienced as painful.[25] Even though we may see the silver lining in the cloud, it may take us some time to get over our painful experience; only as we learn that the change was helpful do we move into Step One of the journey.

The next period in the "Development of Trust" section is clearly related to Step One: it is "a period of sorting out."[26] Once again we are told this initial period "is always somewhat difficult."[27] The budding teacher of God, in this step, has to learn not only that *some* changes are beneficial, but that they *all* are.[28] He generalizes the lesson of the turning point and begins to transfer it to new situations (sentence 3). Many things that were previously valued will now be seen as hindrances to this learning, and the traveler will realize that he must let them go if he is to go on; this arouses feelings of "fear of loss and sacrifice" (sentence 4). We unlearn fear of sacrifice only gradually; its shadow lingers until the journey is almost done.

People who have newly turned to the spiritual path frequently share one common experience: the old pleasures don't satisfy as much as they used to. That can be very disconcerting. In addition, we may realize that if we are going to pursue this spiritual path there are certain things we ought to give up because they aren't consistent with our new purpose. We may see this as sacrifice. As we travel on we need to recognize that feelings of sacrifice and loss are one tool our ego may use to try to hold us back.

In the first step of the journey, sometimes we really are called upon to give things up. In fact, the Course says, this is not sacrifice. We are not giving up anything of value; we are just recognizing the lack of value that was always there.[29] Friendships we have clung to for years, seeking support for our egos, may begin to drop away. Habits we have valued and thought we enjoyed may pass out of our lives. As long as we perceive these changes as some kind of loss, the period will seem difficult. It is only in Step Two that we begin to realize that giving up the valueless does not bring grief, but a lightness of heart.

We Are in Charge of the Journey

"Having chosen to go that way, you place yourself in charge of the journey, where you and only you must remain."[30] The Holy Spirit is your Guide, but you are the commander in chief. He suggests how you should proceed, always with perfect wisdom better than your own, but you must choose to accept His guidance and follow it. You place yourself in charge and you must remain in charge; the journey begins with your choice and is carried out through continued choices. Nothing is ever forced upon us. Jesus made this point at length earlier in the chapter:

Allen Watson

In an impossible situation, you can develop your abilities to the point where they can get you out of it. You have a Guide to how to develop them, but you have no commander except yourself. This leaves you in charge of the Kingdom, with both a Guide to find it [the Holy Spirit] and a means to keep it [your own mind and its choice]. You have a model to follow [Jesus] who will strengthen your command, and never detract from it in any way. You therefore retain the central place in your imagined enslavement, which in itself demonstrates that you are not enslaved.[31]

The decision-making power of our own mind starts us on the journey and also demonstrates its major lesson: that we are not enslaved, but free, and completely responsible for our thoughts. We have a Guide and we have a model, but only we can make the choices required for the journey.

In this first step, by making a choice to see things differently we have placed ourselves in charge. Without realizing it we have demonstrated that we *already are* free. At the beginning we don't realize what we have done; we don't see all the implications. Becoming aware of the power of our own minds and reclaiming our power of decision is a major learning goal of Phase One. All of the sections in the Course that deal with the power of decision and emphasize our responsibility to choose are aspects of Phase One's curriculum. These lessons prepare us for Phase Two, in which we will consistently *exercise* our mind's power.

The temptation at this step is to resist this lesson. As the difficulties arise, we want to blame God for them. "Where is all the joy You promised?" we may ask, or, "Why don't you take away my fears?" His answer, as given in the Course, may seem cruel to our befuddled mind:

The correction of fear *is* your responsibility. When you ask for release from fear, you are implying that it is not.[32]

I would hardly help you if I depreciated the power of your own thinking. This would be in direct opposition to the purpose of this course.[33]

If God intervened it would undermine the purpose of the Course, which is to teach us our mind's power. The whole journey is about the healing of our minds. We need to learn that it is our allegiance to the ego thought system that has made the world we see, and only a change in thought, a change at the level of cause, will be able to change the effects in the visible world.

At the start we believe in our own powerlessness. In Phase One we are learning how untrue powerlessness is. We are responsible for what we see. We are learning that only our own thoughts cause us pain.

> It is your thoughts alone that cause you pain. Nothing external to your mind can hurt or injure you in any way. There is no cause beyond yourself that can reach down and bring oppression. No one but yourself affects you.[34]

That is the down side of being in charge of the journey and acknowledging the power of my own decision. Yet if I cannot accept the responsibility for the mess I have made, I cannot make use of my own mind's power to choose again. When I do acknowledge that no one but myself affects me, however, I can go on to realize the up side of the issue:

> But it is you who have the power to dominate all things you see by merely recognizing what you are.[35]

Learning the universal truth of our power of decision, however, takes time. We are likely to see ourselves as in control in very small areas at first, with most of our life, as we perceive it, still being dictated by outside influences and unwanted thoughts.

> I rule my mind, which I alone must rule….At times it does not seem I am its king at all. It seems to triumph over me, and tell me what to think, and what to do and feel.[36]

Gradually we begin to realize that the principle can be generalized, and holds true wherever we apply it: we are in charge of the journey. Our progress depends, therefore, on nothing but our own willingness, just as our lack of progress stems from our *un*willingness.

When we completely accept that the decision is wholly our own we have shifted from Phase One to Phase Two of the journey. In Phase One our mind goes back and forth, vacillating. Sometimes we say "yes" to God; other times we say "no" to God and "yes" to the ego. Eventually we realize that "'yes' must mean 'not no.'"[37] If we are not consistently happy it *must* be that we are deciding against happiness.

We finally realize that, "You *have* control of this"[38] —that what we want determines what we see, and our decision alone controls the outcome. This lesson of our mind's power, begun in this first step, continues to expand throughout the entire journey until its very end.

The Initial Step Increases Conflict

> This step may appear to exacerbate conflict rather than resolve it, because it is the beginning step in reversing your perception and turning it right-side up. This conflicts with the upside-down perception you have not yet abandoned, or the change in direction would not have been necessary.[39]

Our perception is upside-down. Our way of thinking is wrong-minded. That is precisely why a change in direction is necessary. When you introduce a thought of truth into an upside-down mind, of course it seems to increase your mental conflict. The new idea is diametrically opposed to everything you have taught yourself. The reality hinted at by the experience of a miracle will turn your world upside-down if you accept it. So naturally, conflict seems to increase.

The initial lesson "seems to contain a contradiction, since it is being learned by a conflicted mind."[40] "How can giving be the way to having something?" we ask in confusion. Having seems to be the opposite of giving. So even though we may comprehend the lesson intellectually, we also doubt it, and our motivation becomes conflicted. "For a time, then, he [the learner] is receiving conflicting messages and accepting both."[41] The introduction of a spiritual thought seems to initiate a conflict between the ego and the Holy Spirit, and the battle rages in our own minds. Actually the perception of conflict is all on the ego's side; the Holy Spirit is not at war with anything.

Rather than bringing about peace of mind, which is one of the stated goals of the Course, the beginning steps may seem to destroy your peace of mind completely. "If you accept two thought systems which are in complete disagreement, peace of mind is impossible."[42] In Step One we still *are* accepting two thought systems.

One symptom of such mental conflict, a symptom so wide-spread it could be considered an epidemic, is that we begin to condemn ourselves as "bad" or incompetent spiritual seekers. The Apostle Paul expresses this mental state very well in the New Testament:

For the good that I wish, I do not do; but I practice the very evil that I do not wish….Wretched man that I am! Who will see me free?[43]

Aware as never before of an alternative way of thinking, we feel more ego-dominated than ever. We may respond to this conflict by trying to suppress it or running away from it. We attempt to deny our dark thoughts and to pretend they do not exist; we try to lose ourselves in spiritual highs, run desperately from one spiritual workshop to another, or struggle feverishly against our "sinful" impulses. We frantically seek for experiences of light without being willing to look at our own darkness that is hiding it from us. Or, conversely, we may try to push the *spiritual* side out of awareness and lose ourselves in empty entertainment or in mundane work. I can't begin to tell you how many hours of watching TV and reading science fiction novels were, in my own life, vain attempts to muffle the sounds of conflict in my mind, nor how many days and nights I spent lost in my secular job as a workaholic, trying not to be aware of God's unending call, marking time in my spiritual journey.

The conflict cannot be ignored, suppressed, or run away from. There is only one way out: through the conflict. The dark thoughts must be brought into the presence of the light. Turn to the Holy Spirit and let Him lead you through the conflict. You would condemn yourself for the dark thoughts in your mind; He will not condemn, He will bring forgiveness and healing.

It is extremely important for us, as learners, to anticipate this conflict and discomfort, and to recognize what is happening when it happens. Nothing is wrong. The sense of discomfort and conflict is to be expected when a sudden change is introduced into the mind. The only way out of the conflict is to continue the journey; not to suppress the dichotomy of mind, but to recognize it, bring it into sharp focus, and end it with a firm choice for the truth.

The Ring of Fear

Conflicting motives always generate a certain amount of fear,[44] so the initial step will involve fear as well as conflict. The growing awareness of the ego's dark thoughts within our own minds naturally induces a certain fear. This fear arises as soon as we begin to penetrate beyond the level of purely physical sight, and begin to see with spiritual vision.

The circle of fear lies just below the level the body sees, and seems to be the whole foundation on which the world is based.[45]

When we brush past the layer of distraction that has been hiding spirit from us, we encounter something wonderful. But we also encounter this "circle of fear," the hidden motivations of the ego which have been holding our illusions of the world in place, motivations that have been hiding behind those very illusions.

It is as if, when we get a flash of light, we ask ourselves, "Why haven't I seen this before?" And when we allow our minds to investigate, we discover that the reason is our own egos—something we don't want to admit. We are terrified:

> Here are all the illusions, all the twisted thoughts, all the insane attacks, the fury, the vengeance and betrayal that were made to keep the guilt in place, so that the world could rise from it and keep it hidden.[46]

Yet the Holy Spirit does not intend to frighten us, although fright is nearly universal at this stage. He wants to lead us beyond the fear to the light our fear is hiding. The fear comes not from Him but from ourselves. Fear is a scarecrow we have erected in our minds to keep us from looking at the truth. Many people at this point are so terrified by the scarecrow that they turn back. Knowing in advance that the terror will probably arise, and where it comes from, we can learn to turn instead to the Holy Spirit, asking Him to lead us past the fear.

> Yet God can bring you there, if you are willing to follow the Holy Spirit through seeming terror, trusting Him not to abandon you and leave you there. For it is not His purpose to frighten you, but only yours. You are severely tempted to abandon Him at the outside ring of fear, but He would lead you safely through and far beyond.[47]

It is only natural, when we look within our own minds and find the guilt we have hidden and the ego's murderous thoughts which we have denied, that we are appalled and even frightened by what we find. The ego tries very hard to convince us that the terror of what we will find is sufficient reason to avoid looking within altogether. We do not want to face just how awful the thoughts of our own minds seem to be.

Jesus, in the Course, does not try to hide the fact that we won't like what we first find; in fact he emphasizes it and assures us that the Holy Spirit "will lead us safely through" that ring of fear and beyond. In Workbook Lesson 70 Jesus says that he himself will hold our hand and lead us through.[48]

There is virtually no escaping it. Nearly everyone who begins to work seriously with the Course encounters this wall of resistance just below the surface. The ring of fear is the reason for all the stories you hear about people who start the Course and then throw it away (or give it away, which seems a bit more spiritual). We are tempted to set the Course aside because we associate the fear with the Course, or with God, instead of recognizing that it comes from ourselves. Indeed, if the fear is excessive, it may be advisable to set the Course aside for a time, or to take it in very small doses, until we learn to handle the fear. Fear seems to be something that we must go through in order to press on with the journey; it is an expected part of this first stage of the journey through split-mindedness.

Eventually, we need to realize that we are actively choosing the fear in order to keep ourselves from moving on. Our ego does not want us to see the gifts that lie beyond the fear.

> You cower fearfully lest you should feel Christ's touch upon your shoulder, and perceive His gentle hand directing you to look upon your gifts. How could you then proclaim your poverty in exile? He would make you laugh at this perception of yourself.[49]

There is a marvelous description of this part of the journey in *The Song of Prayer*, in the section on "Praying for Others":

> Guilt must be given up, and not concealed. Nor can this be done without some pain, and a glimpse of the merciful nature of this step may for some time be followed by a deep retreat into fear. For fear's defenses are fearful in themselves, and when they are recognized they bring their fear with them.[50]

The "glimpse of the merciful nature of this step" describes the initial lesson by which we enter the first stage of the journey. But as the Spirit begins to teach us to generalize that lesson to other areas of life, the "glimpse…may for some time be followed by a deep retreat into fear." Why? Because the defenses fear has erected are "fearful in themselves." When we begin to recognize the extent of our denial and projection and the devious means the ego has used to deflect guilt onto others, what is exposed is fearful in itself, and we hide our faces from it, unwilling to look upon our defiled altar.[51] But look we must, that we may bring it to the Holy Spirit for healing, and see beyond it to the reality of Who we really are.

Guilt May Seem to Increase

We are making our first steps at withdrawing blame from the outside world. We have begun to recognize that it is not the world outside us that is causing our problems; the source of the problems lies in the choices of our own minds.

> *Only you can deprive yourself of anything.* Do not oppose this realization, for it is truly the beginning of the dawn of light....This is a crucial step in the reawakening. The beginning phases of this reversal are often quite painful, for as blame is withdrawn from without, there is a strong tendency to harbor it within. It is difficult at first to realize that this is exactly the same thing, for there is no distinction between within and without.[52]

Once again we see that "the beginning phases...are often quite painful." No wonder Jesus says this is a crucial step! It is so easy to be scared off, especially by something like a crushing weight of guilt. As we take these first tentative steps, when we are suddenly overwhelmed with guilt feelings we may wonder, "Am I doing the right thing? Can anything that seems to increase my guilt be a move in the right direction?"

As we begin to stop blaming things outside us for our problems, the tendency is to blame ourselves instead. In fact, the self-blame came first, and was so unbearable we denied it and projected it outside, onto the world. Now, we are withdrawing our projection. What *seems* to be a new flood of self-blame is in reality not new at all; we are simply becoming aware of the guilt we have been repressing all our lives. We have hidden the guilt from ourselves by seeing it in others; when we stop seeing it in others, we become aware of it within us. The journey the Course is taking us on is not increasing guilt, it is revealing it in order to heal it.

What is true of guilt is also true of the fear and discomfort in general. None of it is new. It has always been there. We have just taken off the muffler and have become aware of our resistance to the spirit:

> The strain of refusing faith to truth is enormous, and far greater than you realize.
>
> …The strain of not responding to His call seems to be greater than before. This is not so. Before, the strain was there, but you attributed it to something else.[53]

Our temptation is to revert to blaming the world once again, or even to blaming God and the Course itself. One fellow said to me, "I stopped reading the Course because it made me feel too guilty." Not so. The Course does expose our guilt, but the guilt has always been there. It exposes it to heal it. We have to become aware of the problem before the Answer offered by the Course is meaningful to us.

Another very effective ego diversion is this: Instead of running away from the guilt, we wallow in it. We let the guilt drag us down into a pit of despair until we come to feel that we are hopeless, unable to learn the Course. Often this can seem to be a holy attitude, a noble recognition of our unworthiness. We think it is humility; the Course calls it arrogance!

> [Your judgment] may be so distorted that you believe I was mistaken in choosing you. I assure you this is a mistake of your ego. Do not mistake it for humility.[54]
>
> Do not be arrogant and say you cannot learn His Own curriculum. His Word says otherwise.[55]

The solution is not to retreat back into projection, blaming the world for our ills. The solution is to bring the guilt to the Atonement; to ask for healing. It is to recognize that "blame must be undone, not seen elsewhere."[56] Or as *The Song of Prayer* puts it, "Guilt must be given up, and not concealed."[57] Our inner guilt is an illusion. God does not condemn us; we have invented our own imprisonment, and we can let it go. We can stop crucifying ourselves, and learn instead to love ourselves with the Love of Christ, "for so does your Father love you."[58]

This Step May Take a Long Time

This "very preliminary" step is, nevertheless, one that may take us a long time to get through.

> Some remain at this step for a long time, experiencing
> very acute conflict. At this point they may try to accept
> the conflict, rather than take the next step towards its
> resolution.[70]

Our egos don't give up without a fight. What we are prone to do, the Course says here, is to "accept the conflict." In other words, we just figure that this mental dichotomy is something we have to live with, and we try to adjust. Egos are very good at adjusting.

Dissociation is one of the ego's primary methods for coping with the conflict between the thoughts introduced by the Holy Spirit and the ego's thoughts. "Dissociation is a distorted process of thinking whereby two systems of belief which cannot coexist are both maintained."[71] The thoughts are simply kept apart from each other. We have a saying for it: "I don't let my left hand know what my right hand is doing." So when we want to choose to listen to the ego, to be angry, judgmental, and attacking, we temporarily block the Holy Spirit's thoughts out of awareness. We don't bring them into association with what we are doing; that's dissociation. Conversely, when we want to feel "holy" we wall off our attack thoughts and deny that we have them.

A split mind filled with conflicting motives is the opposite of a mind at peace within itself, which is our goal. The healing for this conflicted condition is to allow the conflicting thoughts to come together. Like darkness and light, when the mutually incompatible thoughts meet in our minds, the dark thoughts will disappear. That is part of the process we must go through to move on from this conflicted stage. We must be willing to "bring…all [our] dark and secret thoughts to Him, and look upon them with Him."[72] We need to bring the darkness into the light; that is the only way it can be healed.

In "The Lessons of the Holy Spirit," Jesus points out that the reason we remain in conflict for so long is because we are afraid to take the next step. We are afraid to bring the ego's thoughts into the open and let them be healed because it seems like giving up part of ourselves. At the same time, we cannot silence the Holy Spirit's Voice; it becomes increasingly clearer, and it is impossible for us not to listen.[73]

It says also, "The way out of conflict between two opposing thought systems is clearly to choose one and relinquish the other."[74]

That is pretty obvious if you even think about it at all. So the way to move beyond Phase One is to make a clear choice for the Holy Spirit, and to relinquish the ego. Step One makes the need for a choice evident. Step Two will involve increasing motivation to make that clear choice, and increasing our willingness to do so. The speed with which we move into that step depends completely on our willingness.

Acting on Faith

There is a fascinating comment made about why the beginning step is so difficult:

> Still strongly aware of the ego in yourself, and responding primarily to the ego in others, you are being taught to react to both as if what you do believe is not true.[75]

The beginning step, then, could be seen as a period in which we are called upon to act on faith—faith that what we see of our own ego, and what we see as the ego in others, is not true. We are being asked to "give all to all" even while our eyes seem to be showing us both our inability to do so and the unworthiness of those to whom we are giving. Although we see attack coming at us, we are asked to react as if it were not attack at all.

> The miracle is taken first on faith, because to ask for it implies that the mind has been made ready to conceive of what it cannot see and does not understand. Yet faith will bring its witnesses to show that what it rested on is really there. And thus the miracle will justify your faith in it, and show it rested on a world more real than what you saw before; a world redeemed from what you thought was there.[76]

The new idea so recently entered into our mind comes, at first, without evidence of its truth. The idea has entered, and we have been made ready to conceive of something we cannot yet see. We are asked, then, to put the idea to the test. We are asked to try it out on faith, to be willing to react to apparent attack or unloving behavior as if it were not true. And this passage says that, if we are willing to do that, "the miracle will justify your faith in it." The evidence of its truth will be there. That evidence is what becomes the impetus that moves us into the next phase.

The evidence may be physical, but more frequently it is simply increasing joy and increasing inner peace. As we place our trust in the Holy Spirit, impossible situations in relationships resolve miraculously, and we know that something has been operating that we have previously been unaware of. The Voice within us is strengthened as we share it, by extending forgiveness and love to our brothers.[77] "The Holy Spirit is invisible, but you can see the results of His Presence, and through them you will learn that He is there."[78]

If you hide nothing, confront the conflicts in your mind, and bring the darkness into the light, you will be healed. Nothing can motivate a person like release from guilt. When the burden of years rolls off your shoulders you feel an incredible lightness of being. You will know you have experienced a miracle, and you will want more.

As you see and experience the results of your faith, your appreciation of the rewards of God will grow deeper and deeper. You will want to align your mind with the Spirit more and more. When you have shifted from simply entertaining the new thought system to actively preferring it to the ego, you will have entered the area of the second lesson of the Holy Spirit (Step Two).

---

[1] T-29.VII.1:6-7

[2] W-pII.333.1:1-4

[3] The second complete description is "The Development of Trust" in Section 4 of the Manual for Teachers. The other sections on which I have drawn heavily for this description of the journey are: "The Altar of God" (T-2.III.3-4); "The Escape from Darkness" (T-1.IV.1); "Reversing Effect and Cause" (T-28.II.8-12); "I am entrusted with the gifts of God" (W-pI.166); and the discussion of the ladder of prayer in *The Song of Prayer*, Chapter 1, "Prayer."

[4] T-6.In.1:7

[5] T-6.V(A).6:1

[6] T-6.V(A).5:13

[7] T-28.III.1:2

[8] T-1.V.3:6

[9] T-6.V(C).6:1

[10] W-pI.108.9:1-3

[11] T-6.V(A).6:2

[12] T-6.V(A).6:1

[13] T-6.V(B).3:9

[14] T-20.VII.2:1

[15] T-17.V.2:5-6

[16] T-17.V.3:2-3

[17] T-17.V.3:8

[18] T-17.V.5:1-4

[19] T-17.V.2:5

[20] M-4.1(A).3-4

[21] M-4.I.2:3

[22] M-4.I(A).3:3

[23] M-4.I(A).3:4

[24] M-4.I(A).3:7-8

[25] M-4.I(A).3:2

[26] M-4.I(A).4:1
[27] M-4.I(A).4:2
[28] M-4.I(A).4:5-6
[29] M-4.I(A).3:3
[30] T-6.V(A).6:3
[31] T-6.IV.9:3-7
[32] T-2.VI.4:1-2
[33] T-2.VII.1:5-6
[34] W-pI.190.5:1-4
[35] W-pI.190.5:6
[36] W-pII.236.Heading, 1:2-3
[37] T-21.VII.12:4
[38] T-21.VII.9:3
[39] T-6.V(A).6:4-5
[40] T-6.V(B).3:6
[41] T-6.V(B).4:6
[42] T-6.V(B).5:2
[43] Romans 7:19, 24, NASB
[44] See "Fear and Conflict," T-2.VI
[45] T-18.IX.4:1
[46] T-18.IX.4:2
[47] T-18.IX.3:7-9
[48] W-pI.70.9:2-4
[49] W-pI.166.8:1-3
[50] S-1.III.4:1-3
[51] See also T-2.V.8:1-5, esp. 8:4
[52] T-11.IV.4:1-2, 4-6
[53] T-17.VIII.3:7, 4:1-3
[54] T-4.IV.10:5-7
[55] M-14.5:11-12
[56] T-11.IV.5:3
[57] S-1.III.4:1
[58] T-11.IV.6:4
[59] T-V(A).2:2, 3:3
[60] T-6.V(A).1:1, 4
[61] T-6.V(A).2:4
[62] T-6.V(A).2:6
[63] T-6.V(A).3:2
[64] T-6.V(A).1:2
[65] T-6.V(A).1:2
[66] T-6.V(A).1:3
[67] T-6.V(A).1:1
[68] T-2.V.7:1
[69] T-2.V.8:2-4
[70] T-6.V(A).6:6-7
[71] T-14.VII.4:3
[72] T-14.VII.6:8
[73] T-6.V(B).4:5
[74] T-6.V(B).5:1
[75] T-6.V(B).3:10
[76] W-pII.13.4:1-3
[77] T-5.III.4:1-3
[78] T-12.VII.3:1

Chapter 5

Escaping from Darkness: Phase One, Step Two

Growing Preference for the New Thought System

If the description of Step Two in this chapter seems to contain many of the same elements as Step One, that is because Step Two extends everything that began in Step One. Step One is merely the beginning of a new thought system; in Step Two, we develop a growing preference for that new way of thinking. The work of Step Two is complete when that preference has advanced to a single-minded decision to allow only the Thought of God in our minds.

A passage we quoted a few pages ago[1] points out that some of us remain in Step One a long time because we try to accept our mental conflict, the conflict between the thought systems of the ego and of the Holy Spirit. The key to moving into Step Two, then, seems to lie in a *refusal* to accept the conflict, a realization that a choice is necessary, and a determination to move on to resolving the conflict. "The way out of conflict between two opposing thought systems is clearly to choose one and relinquish the other."[2]

The conflict begins to dissolve when we begin to recognize our preference for the thoughts of the Holy Spirit. Instead of accepting that we will be forever split-minded, forever in conflict, we realize that we prefer one thought system over the other.

Diminishing Conflict

Although the second step begins the move away from conflict, it does not remove conflict entirely.

The first step...is really only the beginning of the thought reversal. The second step is a positive affirmation of what you want. This, then, is a step in the direction out of conflict, since it means that alternatives have been considered, and one has been chosen as more desirable. Nevertheless, the term "more desirable" still implies that the desirable has degrees. Therefore, although this step is essential for the ultimate decision, it is clearly not the final one.[3]

In Step Two you have begun to move out of conflict, but you aren't out yet. You *prefer* the Holy Spirit to the ego, but sometimes you still choose for the ego quite willingly. To say the thoughts of the Holy Spirit are "more desirable" implies that you still find something desirable in the ego, although less desirable, perhaps, than the Holy Spirit and His thought system. In Step Two you are aware that ultimately you have to choose one or the other completely, and you are moving towards the choice for the Holy Spirit. But you are still clinging to large chunks of the ego system, not wholly willing to let them go, and you are still unaware of the depths of your attachment to separation.

This is the stage where the lesson being learned is that "'yes' must mean 'not no.'"[4] We haven't learned that lesson yet, but we are in the process of learning it. In Step Two we have said "yes" to the Holy Spirit but we haven't yet said a firm "no" to the ego.

Mythology and the Bible are filled with examples of this state of mind. Eurydice, rescued from the underworld by Orpheus, looks back. Lot's wife, escaping from the destruction raining down on Sodom and Gomorrah, looks back and is turned into a pillar of salt. (Thank goodness the God of the Course isn't like that! There would be no shortage of salt among Course students.) The children of Israel, escaping from the darkness of Egypt and having miraculously crossed the Red Sea, spend forty years in the wilderness dabbling with idols, whining about the leeks, onions and garlic they left behind in Egypt, and complaining of the monotony of manna from heaven, unable, therefore, to enter the Promised Land.

In Step Two we are like a girl just engaged who hasn't yet learned that it won't work to date old boyfriends. We know what we want, but we haven't yet fully decided that we *don't want* what we are leaving

Allen Watson

behind. During this step we must learn that lesson. Sometimes it is painful. Sometimes the only way we can learn it is to make the mistakes and suffer the consequences.

> I am teaching you to associate misery with the ego and joy with the spirit. You have taught yourself the opposite. You are still free to choose, but can you really want the rewards of the ego in the presence of the rewards of God?[5]

> His Voice will teach you how to distinguish between pain and joy, and will lead you out of the confusion you have made.[6]

When we choose the ego we are miserable. In Step Two we are still learning that lesson, and there is still an ongoing conflict in our minds. It gradually decreases as, more and more, we bash our heads against the wall and realize we've been heading in the wrong direction again. We begin to learn to turn around *before* we hit the wall.

A Period of Relinquishment

The Manual for Teachers describes this step as a "period of relinquishment."[7] Having realized we prefer the rewards of God, we begin to relinquish the "rewards" of the ego. Sometimes we do this reluctantly.

> If this is interpreted as giving up the desirable, it will engender enormous conflict. Few teachers of God escape this distress entirely. There is, however, no point in sorting out the valuable from the valueless unless the next obvious step is taken [actually giving up the valueless].[8]

"Enormous conflict" can still occur in Step Two if we see what is being asked of us as sacrifice of something desirable. As we begin to learn about special love relationships, for example, hearing that they are the ego's chief weapon for keeping us from Heaven,[9] and recognizing that we are being asked to give all special relationships over to the control of the Holy Spirit, we are likely to feel we are being asked to sacrifice something valuable. We have for so long believed that special love was of great value, it is hard to let it go. "Few teachers of God escape this distress entirely."

It can be anything, any promised reward of the ego, that entices us. Perhaps the promise of financial success may draw our attention from our true goal. Perhaps recognition for our worldly achievements is what entices us. Even though we have moved beyond the confusion of Step One, we still divide our loyalty, and we may have painful lessons of relinquishment to learn.

We may feel that we are "called upon to sacrifice [our] own best interests on behalf of truth."[10] This can happen more than once. Never mind that sacrificing our best interests on behalf of truth is *impossible*; we can't learn that until we truly do give up the valueless. Only then do we discover that the anticipated grief manifests, not as grief, but as "a happy lightheartedness instead; where he thought something was asked of him, he finds a gift bestowed on him."[11]

As we follow the Holy Spirit's guidance in learning relinquishment, instead of sacrifice we find we are learning to "travel light and journey lightly."[12] By letting go, expecting sacrifice, we learn that what we thought was sacrifice is a gift instead. It is no sacrifice to give what we cannot keep to gain what we cannot lose. By relinquishing what is only temporal we rediscover "the one thing that is wholly true and wholly yours,"[13] our eternal Identity in God. "Is it a sacrifice to give up nothing, and to receive the Love of God forever?"[14]

In this step we are learning that, "You do not really want the world you see, for it has disappointed you since time began."[15] We are discovering that, to attain the real world, we have to be willing to learn that the world we have made is false.[16]

Until we learn this lesson, the mental conflict typical of Phase One will remain with us.

> Until you realize you give up nothing, until you understand there is no loss, you will have some regrets about the way that you have chosen. And you will not see the many gains your choice has offered you.[17]

Letting Go of Attack

Learning that "attack cannot *be* justified"[18] is a part of this period also. Attack is the method the ego uses to achieve its goals, so it is only natural that, as ego goals go, attack goes with them.

Wrong-mindedness believes in attack. It believes we are being attacked and therefore can justly attack in return. By attacking we are teaching attack. Therefore, the second lesson of the Holy Spirit, our lesson in Step Two, is: "To Have Peace, Teach Peace to Learn It."[19] The first three words indicate our realization that we *want* peace; that we *prefer and value* peace. To have peace, we have to teach peace, which means that we have to stop teaching attack. How can we have peace while we are teaching attack?

Nor can we get away with teaching *both* peace and attack, which is what we inevitably do at first. "If you teach both, which you will surely do as long as you accept both, you are teaching conflict and learning it."[20] During Step Two we are gradually learning that the ego and the Holy Spirit cannot coexist in our minds. We cannot have both. As the Course often admonishes us, we cannot make exceptions. We have to forgive everyone, not just the ones that are easy. We have to relinquish attack as a method in every case, not just in most cases.

We have to learn to "teach only one lesson."[21] That is the meaning of : "Teach only love, for that is what you are."[22] We do not need attack to be safe; "the only safety lies in extending the Holy Spirit."[23] A few sentences later the Course says that safety lies in "the complete relinquishment of attack,"[24] for relinquishing attack and extending the Holy Spirit are opposite sides of the same coin.

Learning We Have No Enemies

Another way of looking at the relinquishment of attack, or the lesson that "attack cannot be justified," is to say we are learning that we have no enemies. Instead of seeing my brother as an enemy I come to see that he is part of me; to attack him is to attack myself. The Text tells us that we cannot remember our oneness with God as long as we believe that attack of any kind means anything.[25] It then goes on to show how attack is impossible unless we see ourselves as separate:

> It [attack] is unjustified in any form, because it has no meaning. The only way it could be justified is if you and your brother were separate from the other, and all were separate from your Creator....Attack is neither safe nor dangerous. It is impossible. And this is so because the universe is one....
>
> Only the different can attack.[26]

If we are one, attack is impossible. The only way I can justify attacking you is to believe that you are separate from myself, and different from me. So part of learning that attack cannot be justified is learning that we are not separate and different, not enemies, we are one and the same.

The Song of Prayer says that the transition from Step One to Step Two begins with this very lesson:

> *What I have asked for for my brother is not what I would have. Thus have I made of him my enemy.*[27]

In Step Two we begin to recognize that we have "made" people into our enemies; that is not what they are in truth. Giving up the concept of enemies may seem dangerous, and so we may put it off for a long time, thus remaining at the conflict level of Phase One. Once you look at the issue openly, however, it becomes self-evident that we cannot let go of attack and still believe in enemies; they are the same thing.

I Am Doing This

The more we trace our problems back to our own mind's deluded allegiance to the ego, recognizing that nothing outside the mind is the cause, the more it begins to dawn upon us that, "This is not done to me, but *I* am doing this."[28] This is the recognition that shifts us fully into Phase Two of the journey, the pathway of mental vigilance. One situation after another teaches us the lesson that we are responsible for what we see; eventually we recognize the general principle that we are responsible for all our thoughts.

> Nothing beyond yourself can make you fearful or loving, because nothing *is* beyond you. Time and eternity are both in your mind, and will conflict until you perceive time solely as a means to regain eternity. You cannot do this as long as you believe that anything happening to you is caused by factors outside yourself.[29]

Learning that "I am doing this," that "I *am* responsible for what I see,"[30] is a major lesson of Step Two, preparing us for the next step, in which we consciously take responsibility for what we think. When we enter Phase Two we have recognized that time is just a means for regaining eternity; there is no goal in time itself that is worthy of our dedicated attention. Time is useful only as a means to escape time. We cannot learn this until we learn that nothing in time has power to make us happy or sad. To learn that, we must realize deeply, through repeated experiences that prove it to us, that nothing that happens to us is caused by factors outside ourselves. Without that lesson, firmly grasped, time and eternity will continue to conflict in our minds. We will have divided loyalties, divided goals.

In Step Two we are still learning that mind is the cause; the world is the effect. Through the experiences in this step we will come to realize that the only effort that merits our full attention is the reclamation of our minds, watching them carefully to locate and uproot every thought that leads us away from the Kingdom.

Forgiveness

If we combine the last two points, we have forgiveness as the Course teaches it. I do not have enemies. In other words, no one is doing it to me. Instead, I am doing it to myself. Forgiveness, in the Course, teaches us that what we think our brother did to us has not occurred.[31] There was no attack from outside; it was our perception, within our own minds, that was flawed.

Earlier in this book I referred to a passage in the Text, Chapter 2, the third section. The fourth paragraph talks about spiritual vision and how it works to help dissolve the conflict. Spiritual vision sees past what the eyes see, sees past both the errors of my brother's ego and my own errors. It "looks within and recognizes immediately that the altar has been defiled and needs to be repaired and protected."[32] It does not see the error as "sin." Instead, it recognizes the call for help behind it, the spiritual "altar" that needs repair and protection, both in myself and my brother. This recognition brings the mind into the service of spirit, willing to choose to love instead of to attack, to heal instead of destroy, to forgive instead of condemn. Spiritual vision lets us see that forgiveness is justified, and attack is not. In Step Two we are learning forgiveness, which is another way of saying we become increasingly aware that attack is not justified.

Ending Specialness

Unforgiveness separates. Forgiveness makes way for joining. When we forgive our brother we are able to recognize our common interests, our common will for wholeness. Forgiveness transforms a brother from an enemy into a friend, a fellow traveler, someone with whom we can join and collaborate in going home to God. The more we take responsibility for our perceptions and learn forgiveness, the more we find ourselves drawn together with others in the common purpose of returning home.

That is the basis of a holy relationship. In Phase One of the journey we are dealing for the most part with our individual perceptions. Through forgiveness we begin to transcend that individual phase, and to ready ourselves for Phase Two, in which we join with others in fulfilling our function and finding our way home—together.

> Would it be possible for you to hate your brother if you were like him? Could you attack him if you realized you journey with him, to a goal that is the same? Would you not help him reach it in every way you could, if his attainment of it were perceived as yours? You are his enemy in specialness; his friend in a shared purpose.[33]

Through forgiveness we are learning in this stage of our journey to end the perception of differences and specialness. We do not have different goals; our goal is the same as our brother's goal. His reaching the goal *is* our reaching it. Competition is unthinkable; our journeys are inextricably linked.

Entering this step we do not believe in our sameness; we believe in differences. We are enmeshed in specialness without knowing how deeply, and we fear our brothers, and fear God because of our specialness.

> The fear of God and of your brother comes from each unrecognized belief in specialness....Every twinge of malice, or stab of hate or wish to separate arises here. For here the purpose that you and your brother share becomes obscured from both of you. You would oppose this course because it teaches you you and your brother are alike.[34]

Resistance to the Course itself arises again in this step as we realize it is telling us, "you and your brother are alike." We begin to find how tenacious the thought is that we are *not* like other people; we are different; we are special. Often there is one particular person about whom the thought, "I am like him," is utterly unacceptable to our minds. We find ourselves thinking, "Oh, no! I am not like that awful person." Learning to let go of specialness, to forgive, and to see the healing of our brother as the healing of ourselves is what Step Two consists of.

Allen Watson

Step Two is a time of uncovering "each unrecognized belief in specialness," realizing its source, and bringing it to the Holy Spirit for healing. We must get beyond "enemy consciousness" before we can move into the next phase, in which we continue the journey together with our brothers.

Letting the Holy Spirit Decide

To become free of conflict, we must learn to listen to only one voice: the Voice of the Holy Spirit. "If you are to be conflict-free yourself, you must learn only from the Holy Spirit and teach only by Him."[35] In Step Two of this first phase we are learning this lesson; in Phase Two we will be applying it, although our application may still be imperfect.

In Step Two we are unlearning the idea that, "it is up to you to decide which voice is true."[36] We are learning that truth is what God created, and our decisions cannot change that truth. We think that it is up to us to decide what is valuable and what is not, but gradually we realize that we cannot make this decision; it has already been made, once and for all, by God.

As you begin to realize the quiet power of the Holy Spirit's Voice, and Its perfect consistency, it must dawn on your mind that you are trying to undo a decision that was irrevocably made for you. That is why I suggested before that you remind yourself to allow the Holy Spirit to decide for God for you.[37]

The way to choose only one thought system is, ironically, to stop trying to choose for ourselves and simply to listen. The only decision we need to make is the decision not to decide for ourselves, because everything has been given to us by God's decision.[38] (Deciding to listen only to the Holy Spirit is equivalent to relinquishing judgment, by the way, since judgment is evaluating and making choices on our own.)

In the first phase of the journey we are still learning this lesson, still only coming to this decision to hear only one Voice. It is because we have not decided that we continue to experience mental conflict. The move into Phase Two comes about largely because we firmly decide to hear only the Voice for God, and to disregard the ego. Step Two is the preparation for that decision, in which we gradually learn the power and perfect consistency of the Holy Spirit's Voice in one situation after another, so that it finally dawns upon us that all our efforts at decision-making are futile, since the decision has already been irrevocably made by God. We cannot decide, for instance, what we are; God made that decision the moment He created us.

It is easy to fool ourselves into believing that we have already made this choice to hear only one Voice. Simply understanding that the choice is inevitable is not equivalent to making the choice. Simply thinking, "I want to hear only one Voice" is not making the decision to do so. Far too easily we can say those words without really meaning them, just as thousands of people may say "I want to lose weight" without ever making a conclusive decision to do so.

Look at the evidence of your life. Are you wholly joyous? Is your mind at peace within itself, free from conflict? Is pain still real in your perception? If what is manifesting in your life is not free from the effects of the ego, your mind is not free from listening to the ego—even if you are not aware of listening.

We learn first to *want* to hear only one Voice. Once we want this we must learn to distinguish that Voice from the voice of the ego. Many students feel frustrated at this point because they cannot easily tell the difference between ego and Holy Spirit. The experiences of Step Two are teaching us how to recognize His Voice, and we need to be at peace while we learn the lessons. We will learn, many times, by making mistakes. Such mistakes are not failure; they are a necessary part of our learning process.

The decision we are being led to here—to hear only one Voice—is a decision of *purpose*. It does not mean that, once we make the decision, we will instantly hear only that Voice; it means that having made the decision, we will now direct our efforts towards carrying it out and manifesting it in our lives. This decision of purpose is like deciding to lose weight; while the decision is crucial, there is still a long period in which we implement the decision. *Implementing* the decision to hear only one Voice is a major component of Phase Two of the journey.

Completing or making that decision wholly—to the point where we actually listen only to the Holy Spirit and never to the ego—is one of the things that tips us over into the real world, the journey's end. Jesus, holding himself up as our model in learning, says that learning to hear *only* the Holy Spirit and no other was "the final lesson" that he learned, which clearly indicates it brings the spiritual journey to its end. In a highly significant sentence he then makes a point that cannot be too strongly emphasized: learning to hear only the Holy Spirit is no trivial task. He tells us (from experience, no doubt) that "it takes effort and great willingness to learn."[39]

> This is still a preliminary step.[40]

> The second step, then, is still perceptual, although it is a giant step toward the unified perception that reflects God's knowing.[41]

The phrase "unified perception that reflects God's knowing" refers to true perception, or the real world, which is the end of the journey. This second step, making a positive affirmation of what we want or a decision of purpose, is clearly essential; it sets the direction for us out of conflict and towards that goal, but it obviously is not the "final decision" that will bring us entry into the real world. In that sense deciding what we want is still preliminary.

Nevertheless it is called "a giant step." Coming to the point at which we consciously *prefer* to hear only the Holy Spirit, or to make peace our only goal, is no small thing. It may often appear that we stumble into Step One almost against our will (although that is impossible, because the goal of the journey *is* our will). We cannot "stumble" through Step Two; what we began to accept almost blindly in our turning point, and in Step One, now becomes our conscious choice. And that is, indeed, a "giant step."

Penetrating the Ego Thought System

Step Two is a period during which we begin to penetrate the layers of the ego thought system, exposing hidden parts and discovering obscured connections, working our way to its core.

> As you take this step and hold this direction, you will be pushing toward the center of your thought system, where the fundamental change will occur.[42]

Clearly this is not anything sudden; we "take this step and hold this direction," which implies a certain persistence on our part, a determination to stay on course. The idea of pushing towards the center carries a hint that, as we move into Step Two, we begin by dealing with issues that are, relatively speaking, on the periphery of our thought system. The first things we notice are the fresh tendrils of the ego, and as we progress we uncover branches, then trunk, then roots. This uncovering of the ego thought system can be an unpleasant experience, but the Course repeatedly says it is absolutely crucial to our journey:[43]

> You may wonder why it is so crucial that you look upon your hatred and realize its full extent.[44]

> Yet we have repeatedly emphasized the need to recognize fear and face it without disguise as a crucial step in the undoing of the ego.[45]

> When you have at last looked at the ego's foundation without shrinking you will also have looked upon ours [the foundation of God and Christ].[46]

We might think of this step as "recognizing the problem." As Phase One progresses, we become increasingly aware that the root of all our problems is within our own minds and not outside us. The problem is our own ego, and the ego is empowered only by our own mind. It is a thought *we* are thinking and nothing else.

We begin the journey believing, no doubt, that we have many problems. As we press towards the center of the ego thought system, however, we begin to trace each problem back to the same root. We must first be willing to recognize that we *do have problems*, that is, that thoughts of fear, anger, attack, rage, jealousy, and separateness are indeed present in our mind. Once we admit to the problem, a solution is possible, because the root problem, the granddaddy of all problems—the problem of separation—has already been solved.

> If you are willing to recognize your problems, you will recognize that you have no problems. Your one central problem has been answered, and you have no other. Therefore, you must be at peace. Salvation thus depends on recognizing this one problem, and understanding that it has been solved. One problem, one solution.[47]

This is what is meant by pressing towards the center of our thought system. In this stage of our journey, we begin to learn, bit by bit, that all the things we thought of as separate and distinct problems, with

Allen Watson

separate and distinct solutions, are all aspects of only one problem: our belief in separation from God. That one problem has one solution: the Atonement, which is the fact that the separation never happened except in our dreams.

As we bring our problems and our darkest secrets into the light, one by one, and bring them to the Atonement, the fear that has always surrounded those problems and secrets melts away.

> As long as you recognize only the need for the remedy, you will remain fearful. However, as soon as you accept the remedy, you have abolished the fear. This is how true healing occurs.[48]

The discomfort of Phase One has a purpose. It makes us aware of the need for a remedy. "Discomfort is aroused only to bring the need for correction into awareness."[49] Once aware of the need, the next step is to accept that remedy; without that, guilt and fear remain. To recognize our fear without accepting the remedy is a step backwards rather than forwards.[50]

One by one, the ego's masks are torn away, and the ugliness beneath is brought to healing. Over and over again we discover that the ego's purpose is always to foster guilt, which keeps us in fear, which in turn keeps us in separation. More and more we come to associate our misery with the ego, and our joy with the release brought to us by the Holy Spirit. The common root of all our problems becomes increasingly evident, increasing our motivation to turn firmly away from its voice, to listen only to the Voice for God.

Learning What We Really Want

In several places, the Course tells us that we do not know our own will. We do not recognize what we really want. We do not know that God's Will and our will are the same.

Step Two is teaching us what we want. It is helping us, through many learning experiences, to begin to recognize that we do not want the ego, and that we do want the spirit. We want our Self as God created it. By one example after another the Holy Spirit is strengthening our motivation until we realize that the peace of God is not only desirable, it is all we want. It is the *only* thing worth living for, the aim we seek, our purpose and our function and our life.[51]

Part of this lesson is learning to recognize all the things we are choosing instead of peace. Can it be possible that how a toothpaste tube is squeezed is more important to me than the peace of God? Yes, indeed; I can be that small-minded. When we recognize the insanity of our choices, we will choose again, because fundamentally we are not insane. Seen clearly the ego is unsupportable and even laughable.

In the second step we stop trying to decide for ourselves and begin to recognize that somewhere deep within we have already decided; we already want peace or we would not have started this difficult journey! The decision has been made for us.[52] We were created wanting peace; we don't have any choice about it.

Recognizing that we want peace, we start to move in that direction. As we give peace, we receive it; as we share it, we experience it. Each experience of peace increases our motivation; we want more of it, and we want it more consistently. During this step of our development we are not always at peace, but we are constantly growing in our desire to have peace, and the frequency of peaceful periods in our lives is increasing as well.

The problem that remains is that while we do desire peace, we do not desire it *wholly*.[53] We cannot yet say that the peace of God is *all* we want; that phrase is more expressive of Step Four than Step Two. Here, in Step Two, we are moving in that direction but we have not arrived yet. Our desire for peace is not unequivocal. There are still things we think we want more than peace, or things we want along with peace that are not compatible with it. To some degree we want to have our cake and eat it too.

It is this single-mindedness that we are learning during Step Two. One by one the idols fall. One by one, we recognize that we *do not want* what we thought we did, and so we come to learn the one thing we truly want, the "pearl of great price" for which we are willing to relinquish everything, even our whole world.

Progress in This Step Is Intermittent

> At the second step progress is intermittent, but the second step is easier than the first because it follows. Realizing that it *must* follow is a demonstration of a growing awareness that the Holy Spirit will lead you on.[54]

It is a progressive thing. The progress during this stage is intermittent. Not "may be" intermittent, "*is*" intermittent. That is, there will be a spurt of progress, then a plateau, then another spurt. We should not be distressed when things seem to level off a while and progress falters. That is simply the way of the journey.

There is no specific reason given in Chapter 6 telling why the progress in Step Two is intermittent, but the reasons are fairly evident. Most of our ego attachments are hidden from our conscious awareness at the start. The ego survives by hiding itself from our awareness, disguising and obscuring its motives. It takes a little while for us to see through the ego deception, and then we need to respond to our new awareness of the problem, bringing it to healing. We can't handle everything at once.

It will seem, as you uncover a major patch of ego and experience healing, that you have arrived at the final lesson, but then another area of attachment to the world will crop up; some aspect of your life where ego values linger, something yet more to which you are clinging, cherishing it above your peace. Once again you will find yourself learning not to seek "what you will surely lose," and to "content yourself with what you will as surely keep."[55] Each such learning leads to another plateau.

The second step is easier because it follows the first step. You have built up some momentum, in other words. The momentum will only increase. One thing that happens as you begin to move on into the second step is that you realize the process you are going through is a necessary process; it "must follow" the first step. Once the Holy Spirit's thoughts have taken root in your mind, the conflict with the ego thought system is inevitable. You must root out every aspect of the ego, with His help, and let them go. Exposing the ego can be disturbing until you realize it is necessary. When you recognize its necessity, you relax a bit. Instead of being disturbed when another area of ego clinging gets exposed, instead of exclaiming, "Oh, no! Not again!" you will realize that the experience does not mean you've fallen back. Rather, it is evidence that the Holy Spirit is leading you on.

You know you are making headway with Step Two when you begin to relax about your own ego. You realize the purification process is necessary, and you are increasingly aware that "the Holy Spirit will lead you on." You don't become distressed when you uncover another aspect of specialness within yourself. Your distress about the ego is something the ego loves; it means you are acknowledging its existence and power. Instead of distress, as this step progresses, you begin to experience a lightheartedness about your ego. You realize that it is powerless and, in the end, meaningless. You smile when you see it rear its ugly head, and perhaps you say to yourself, "So what else is new? I have an ego; big surprise." Rather than trying to deny what is there, you open that formerly darkened area of your mind to the Holy Spirit for His healing.

Being upset about your ego is a major mistake, and one the Course specifically warns us about as we journey home: "Never accord the ego the power to interfere with the journey. It has none, because the journey is the way to what is true."[56]

The Branching of the Road

The mid-point of the journey, the transition between the two phases, is referred to as "the branching of the road."[57] The first part of the journey has shown us enough of the ego for us to realize that we do not want it, and that a clear-cut choice is called for.

> This is a crucial period in this course, for here the separation of you and the ego must be made complete. For if you have the means to let the Holy Spirit's purpose be accomplished, they can be used....You know what your Creator wills is possible, but what you made [the ego] believes it is not so. Now must you choose between yourself and an illusion of yourself. Not both, but one. There is no point in trying to avoid this one decision. It must be made. Faith and belief can fall to either side, but reason tells you misery lies only on one side and joy upon the other.[58]

When this time comes we know it. There is no point in trying to avoid the decision. "It must be made."

> When you come to the place where the branch in the road is quite apparent, you cannot go ahead. [You can't continue as you have before, with divided loyalties.] You must go either one way or the other. For now if you go straight ahead, the way you went before you reached the branch, you will go nowhere. The whole purpose of coming this far was to decide which branch you will take now.[59]

Allen Watson

In truth, the turning point that started the journey placed us at this branch. All the way we seem to have travelled in the first two steps has just made us aware of the branch, aware of the necessity for a clear choice. Now, at last, we see the branch clearly. We have reached the point where "the branch in the road is quite apparent." Until this point we have been able to obscure the choice between our Self and an illusion. Now it is quite clear, and we can't deny the need for decision any longer. We can, however, still delay it:

> No one who reaches this far can make the wrong decision, although he can delay. And there is no part of the journey that seems more hopeless and futile than standing where the road branches, and not deciding on which way to go.[60]

Steps One and Two have been a period of time in which our reasons for delay have been overturned one by one. The branch in the road represents a moment when our mind, free of reasons for delay, is consciously confronted with the choice between ego and spirit. Postponement at this point is particularly pathetic. We know we have to choose, but instead we just stand there at the crossroads, scuffing our feet and looking foolish.

I am utterly certain that within this lifetime I have reached that crossroads several times, and I have no doubt I did the same in previous lives. And each time before I have procrastinated.

I have already referred to the exodus of the Hebrews from Egypt as a picture of the spiritual journey. In that picture, the branching of the road was the point of entering the Promised Land of Canaan. I can recall being particularly smitten by a poem I once ran across. I am sure it stuck in my mind because it spoke strongly to me about myself, and although its dark last line would never fit within the Course's thought system, I still think the poem is representative of us when we come to the branching of the road and hesitate:

> They came to the gates of Canaan,
> But they never entered in.
> They came to the very threshold,
> But they perished in their sin.

In the Course's picture of things, "No one…can make the wrong decision."[61] All we can do is delay the decision. We do so, unfortunately, over and over. We come to the branch in the road and turn back. We decide instead to make one more run through the maze, to pursue one more useless goal. We choose to seek another special relationship, or another career goal. We look for some way to complete ourselves without letting go of the ego.

"Delay does not matter in eternity, but it is tragic in time."[62] So it is tragic when we reach the branching of the road and delay our inevitable decision. The decision is inevitable because it has been already made; we made it when we started on the journey, and it was made in Heaven for us before the journey even began.

> It is but the first few steps along the right way that seem hard, for you have chosen, although you still may think you can go back and make the other choice. This is not so. A choice made with the power of Heaven to uphold it cannot be undone. Your way is decided. There will be nothing you will not be told, if you acknowledge this.[63]

What seems to be a decision at the branching of the road is really just an *acknowledgement* that the choice has already been made. What we are doing is "acknowledging [our] mind as God created it" and "accepting it as it is."[64] We are making the choice to have in our mind only what God put there,[65] and we are choosing to be vigilant to that end. This choice is the start of Phase Two of the journey.

---

[1] T-6.V(A).6:7-8
[2] T-6.V(B).5:1
[3] T-6.V(B).8:2-6
[4] T-21.VII.12:4
[5] T-4.VI.5:6-8
[6] T-7.X.7:3
[7] M-4.I(A).5:1
[8] M-4.I(A).5:2-4
[9] T-16.V.2:3
[10] M-4.I(A).5:5
[11] M-4.I(A).5:8
[12] T-13.VII.13:4
[13] T-13.VII.8:4
[14] T-24.II.6:6
[15] T-13.VII.3:1
[16] T-13.VII.4:4
[17] T-29.II.1:5-6

[18] T-25.III.1:2
[19] T-6.V(B).Heading
[20] T-6.V(B).5:3
[21] T-6.V(B).5:3; T-6.III.2:1
[22] T-6.III.2:4
[23] T-6.III.3:1
[24] T-6.III.3:7
[25] T-22.VI.12:1-2
[26] T-22.VI.12:3-4, 8-10, 13:1
[27] S-1.III.3:5-6
[28] T-28.II.12:5
[29] T-10.In.1:1-3
[30] T-21.II.2:3
[31] W-pII.1.1:1
[32] T-2.III.4:3
[33] T-24.I.6:1-4
[34] T-24.I.8:1, 4-6

35 T-6.III.2:2
36 T-6.V(B).6:3
37 T-6.V(B).6:4-5
38 T-7.X.6:8-9
39 T-5.II.3:10
40 T-6.V(B).8:1
41 T-6.V(B).9:1
42 T-6.V(B).9:2
43 For an in-depth discussion of why uncovering the ego is so crucial, see *Through Fear to Love* in the same series as this book.
44 T-13.III.1:1
45 T-12.I.8:5
46 T-11.In.4:2
47 W-pI.80.1:1-5
48 T-2.VI.8:7-9
49 T-2.V.7:8
50 T-12.I.8:4
51 W-pI.205.1:2-3
52 T-6.V(B).6:4
53 T-6.V(B).8:7
54 T-6.V(B).9:3-4
55 T-13.VII.15:2-3
56 T-8.V.6:4-5
57 T-22.IV.Heading
58 T-22.II.6:1-2, 5-10
59 T-22.IV.1:1-4
60 T-22.IV.1:7-8
61 T-22.IV.1:7
62 T-5:VI.1:3
63 T-22.IV.2:1-5
64 T-6.V(C).5:4-5
65 T-6.V(C).5:4

Chapter 6

Emerging into the Light:
Phase Two

When we enter the second phase of the journey, the way at once becomes easier. This part is what *The Song of Prayer* calls "the quicker ascent."[1] The road from this point on is, if not downhill, at least a gentler slope upwards to the lawns of Heaven.

Of course the way becomes easier. Until now we have been doggedly holding on to two thought systems in our minds. Now we have chosen firmly to accept one (God's) and let the other (ego's) go. The source of most of our distress throughout Phase One has been our own indecision. Now, having recognized the errors of our own mind as the source of the difficulty, we have chosen to clean them up with the help of the Holy Spirit. Instead of choosing *for* conflict, as we have been doing, we have now chosen *against* conflict. We have decided that the conflict is exactly what we do not want. Naturally, this makes for a more peaceful state of mind.

In the first part of the journey we have been mostly identified with our ego, but attracted to spirit and learning the benefits of choosing for spirit. We enter the second half when we have tilted the scale in favor of spirit, realizing this is all we truly want, yet we still must be watchful to protect our minds against the ego's attempts to regain control.

The Course speaks of the later part of the journey in glowing terms, referring to "all the magnificence, the grandeur of the scene and the enormous opening vistas that rise to meet one as the journey continues." It says that the splendor "reaches indescribable heights as one proceeds."[2] We have indeed seen the light at the end of the tunnel, and our pace quickens as we move on, our vision riveted by what we have seen at the end, our hearts uplifted by the attraction of our love for His.

That is why I have called Phase Two "emerging into the light." Phase Two is a much happier time. There is an upsurge of energy as we enter into happy collaboration with the Holy Spirit in uncovering and laying aside every last defense of the ego. We no longer want the defenses and are eager to be rid of them.

> The escape from darkness involves two stages: First, the recognition that darkness cannot hide. This step usually entails fear. Second, the recognition that there is nothing you want to hide even if you could. This step brings escape from fear. When you have become willing to hide nothing, you will not only be willing to enter into communion but will also understand peace and joy.[3]

We enter Phase Two when we have learned that there is nothing we want to hide; no ego darkness which so shames us that we try to hide it from ourselves, the world, and God. We know that bringing it into the light results, not in judgment and condemnation, but in healing and release. We gladly bring our illusions to the truth because we value the peace and joy that always follows our doing so. We live in steadily increasing peace; whenever our minds are not joyous we quickly come for healing.

Step Three: Rest and Joining

Most of the times the Course presents the steps of the journey, what I am calling Steps Three and Four are not separated. Only "Development of Trust" mentions an intermediate step at the beginning of Phase Two. It is called "a period of settling down."[4] It is characterized by two things. First, it is a time of rest and peace. Second, it is a time in which we gather companions for the journey.

A Time of Rest

Once we have learned, through actual relinquishment, that there is no sacrifice, we enter the only period of our journey that "Development of Trust" describes with a positive phrase—a "period of settling down." By this stage we have recognized the existence of another way. We have realized that we prefer the way of the Holy Spirit to that of the ego. Now we have arrived at the point of deciding that this other way, the Kingdom of God and the peace of God, is *all* that we want. "This is a quiet time, in which the teacher of God rests a while in reasonable peace."[5]

> Now he consolidates his learning. Now he begins to see the transfer value of what he has learned. Its potential is literally staggering, and the teacher of God is now at the point in his progress at which he sees in it his whole way out. "Give up what you do not want, and keep what you do." How simple is the obvious! And how easy to do![6]

This can be an almost euphoric period. The basic conflict over what we want has ended. Our minds suddenly become clear, and it all seems so easy and obvious. We have passed the branch in the road. We want God's peace and joy, and only that. All we need to do is to follow the Holy Spirit in rejecting everything that does not foster joy.[7] We see the "transfer value;" we recognize that what we have learned applies to everything. The path now seems self-evident to us, and we wonder how we could ever have been confused about it.

"The teacher of God needs this period of respite."[8] The first phase has been mostly negative: undoing, sorting out, relinquishing. We have gone through fear and through enormous conflict; it has not been an easy journey. Now the conflict seems over. Yet the rest, the euphoria, is to some degree an illusion. "He has not yet come as far as he thinks."[9] Part of the relief we feel at this point is that we think we are almost home, and unfortunately we are mistaken.

There is a temptation when this plateau is achieved to believe that we have finally conquered the spiritual mountain. We think the long journey is over. We do not realize we have reached only the last rest station on the journey, and there is yet a long way to go. At this point, "All that he really learned so far was that he did not want the valueless, and that he did want the valuable."[10] That is a perfect description of what occurs in the second lesson of the Holy Spirit.

All through Phase One we have been torn between the values of the past and the values of what is promised by God. Finally, however, our choice is made.

The third step, then, is a statement of what you want to believe, and entails a willingness to relinquish everything else.[11]

The turmoil of confusion is over. The relief that comes from making this decision is nearly indescribable, and so we rest a while before we go on. It will not take long for us to realize that there is indeed more to do; much, much more. We have only just begun to discover our function as saviors of the world.

We Begin to Remember God

With the conflict mostly over, our minds become very peaceful. This is what the "preliminary" steps of Phase One have been leading up to: a mind at peace within itself. In this state of mind the memory of God can at last arise:

> The memory of God comes to the quiet mind. It cannot come where there is conflict, for a mind at war against itself remembers not eternal gentleness.[12]

The first half of the journey concentrated on removing the blocks to our awareness of Love. The second half, in which our mind is no longer at war against itself, brings with it the memory of God. "You will remember what you know when you have learned you cannot be in conflict."[13]

> Forget not that the motivation for this course is the attainment and keeping of the state of peace. Given this state the mind is quiet, and the condition in which God is remembered is attained.[14]

All that remains is to uncover and discard all remaining thoughts of conflict, for we have learned we do not want them. The experience of this step brings us increasing awareness of the presence of Love everywhere. Our hearts begin to beat more calmly as we free ourselves from the unconscious but constant fear of God. We begin to hear the song of Heaven, so long forgotten. We begin to remember God.

Gathering Our Companions for the Journey

When we are ready to move on, when we realize that the journey is not done, we have great help.

> When he is ready to go on, he goes with mighty companions beside him. Now he rests a while, and

gathers them before going on. He will not go on from here alone.[15]

It says the teacher "gathers" his companions before going on. I believe that this is a clear indication of forming holy relationships. At this point we join with others on the journey, and gather companions for the road; we take the hand of a brother or sister who is travelling the same way, and we agree to travel together. Our holy relationships may *begin* earlier, but it seems to be during this period of rest that these relationships find and accept their function: to go home to God *together*, and to extend holiness to the entire world.

The statement that "he will not go on from here alone" is, I think, not so much a promise as a statement of fact. "The ark of peace is entered two by two."[16] The real world is not entered alone; "the whole new world rests in the hands of every two who enter here to rest."[17] For each of us, our own entry comes as we take someone else with us in holy relationship.

Joined with our companions to give and receive healing, we can begin to fulfill our function. Our mutual dedication to healing is "the beginning of the return to knowledge; the foundation on which God will help build again the thought system you share with Him."[18]

Step Four: Vigilance for God and His Kingdom

In Chapter 6 of the Text, the last step in our journey is called "vigilance for God and His Kingdom."[19] The "Development of Trust" section in the Manual calls this step of the journey a "period of unsettling."[20] The premature relaxation that punctuates the beginning of Phase Two comes to an end; there is more work to do. Step Four is a time of *watchfulness* rather than relaxation. We work and watch, however, not in gloom and sorrow, but with joy.

> How light and easy is the step across the narrow boundaries of the world of fear when you have recognized Whose hand you hold! Within your hand is everything you need to walk with perfect confidence away from fear forever, and to go straight on, and quickly reach the gate of Heaven itself.[21]

Notice that there are two things for which we are vigilant: God, and

His Kingdom. We watch our minds to guard them for God and against the ego; and we enter wholeheartedly into our function as God's saviors to bring salvation to the Sonship, His Kingdom. Each of these two aspects will be discussed in more detail in a moment.

Step Four May Be a Long One

The period of unsettling, of vigilance only for God and His Kingdom, and of joining with others to extend healing, is not a short period. Contrary to what many seem to think, the Course does not lead us to expect instant enlightenment. Once we embark on this stage of the journey, we can be in for a long haul.

> And now he must attain a state [the next stage or period, that of achievement] that may remain impossible to reach for a long, long time. He must learn to lay all judgment aside, and ask only what he really wants in every circumstance. Were not each step in this direction so heavily reinforced, it would be hard indeed![22]

The Song of Prayer says this part of the trip "begins the quicker ascent, but there are still many lessons to learn."[23] We are moving faster, but there is still a long way to go.

Jesus is quite blunt here; this period of vigilance "would be hard indeed" unless each step in this direction were "heavily reinforced." This path is a demanding one, but each small step is heavily reinforced with rewards of peace and joy, with the strength of the Holy Spirit added to our little willingness, and with reminders of the value and certainty of our goal.

Learning "to lay all judgment aside" is no small task. It is the aim of the curriculum: "The aim of our curriculum, unlike the goal of the world's learning, is the recognition that judgment in the usual sense is impossible."[24] We are learning not to judge what we want, but specifically to *refrain* from judging for ourselves and to ask the Holy Spirit to tell us what it is we really want. We are to learn to do this, notice, "in every circumstance." The "long, long" time is usually required to allow us to expand what we have learned and apply it to everyone and everything in the world.

> Yet will you choose in countless situations, and through time that seems to have no end, until the truth be your decision.[25]

We are inclined to feel disheartened by the idea of a "long, long time," "time that seems to have no end," and of "many lessons to learn." Jesus understands our impatience, and often in the Course he stops to remind us that time is only an illusion. When we think, "It would take a miracle to enable me to guard my thoughts so carefully," he reminds us that miracles are what the Course is all about.[26] He tells us repeatedly that the outcome is certain, that we are absolutely guaranteed to finish the journey, and he says, "Those who are certain of the outcome can afford to wait, and wait without anxiety."[27] In this last stage of the journey, we need to learn to travel with patience, realizing that "learning is living here."[28] Certain of the outcome, we are content to carry out our part in the plan of the Atonement, knowing that the last step is in God's Hands, and its timing will be perfect.

In the Manual for Teachers we are told that our progress may be slow or rapid depending on how quickly we learn not to exclude anything from the Atonement. "Sudden and complete awareness" may happen in some cases, "but this is comparatively rare."[29] Then it continues:

> It is only the end that is certain. Anywhere along the way, the necessary realization of inclusiveness may reach him. **If the way seems long, let him be content.** He has decided on the direction he wants to take. What more was asked of him? And having done what was required, would God withhold the rest?[30]

Guarding Our Mind: Vigilance for God

Vigilance seems to be the predominant characteristic of this last part of the journey. We have decided what we want to believe, and now we are watching our minds for contradictory beliefs, eager to let them go. We are vigilant for God, and vigilant against the ego.

The following lines place the lesson in respect to the first two:

> This is a major step toward fundamental change. Yet it still has an aspect of thought reversal, since it implies that there is something you must be vigilant *against*. It has advanced far from the first lesson, which is merely the beginning of thought reversal, and also from the second, which is essentially the identification of what is more desirable. This step, which follows from the second as the

second follows from the first, emphasizes the dichotomy between the desirable and the undesirable. It therefore makes the ultimate choice inevitable.[31]

Dichotomy means "a division into two mutually exclusive, opposed, or contradictory groups."[32] In other words, by entering this step you have clearly identified what you want and distinguished it from what you do not want. You have seen that the ego's goals and the Holy Spirit's goals are mutually exclusive, opposed, and contradictory. You understand that "you cannot see both worlds."[33] You have realized that to be free of conflict, you must have *only one goal*, and that is the peace of God.

Notice the words "fundamental change." What is being referred to here? It is the transition to the real world, the final shift from split-mindedness to right-mindedness, the ultimate choice to hear *only* the Voice for God. That is the goal of the curriculum, the end of the journey through fear to love. Our vigilance in this step is what makes that end inevitable.

Why is our choice to be vigilant only for God still not the fundamental change? Because it still contains an element of a second thought system in the mind; there is something we must be vigilant *against*.[34] We have come a long way to reach this point. *But there are still ego thoughts in our minds.*

> This lesson is unequivocal in that it teaches there must be no exceptions, although it does not deny that the temptation to make exceptions will occur.[35]

The ego will still rear its ugly head. We will be tempted to make exceptions—for instance, to withhold forgiveness from one particular person, or to refuse to let go of judgment in one certain area. That is precisely why the lesson calls for us to "be vigilant." We are vigilant against exceptions. To be vigilant means "keenly watchful to detect danger; wary; ever awake and alert; sleeplessly watchful."[36]

Why is vigilance necessary? Because, although we have consciously decided to hear only one Voice, we still have many unrecognized beliefs in our mind that stem from the ego, unrecognized beliefs in attack and specialness.

> But an unrecognized belief is a decision to war in secret, where the results of conflict are kept unknown and never

brought to reason, to be considered sensible or not....Mistake you not the power of these hidden warriors to disrupt your peace....The secret enemies of peace, your least decision to choose attack instead of love, unrecognized and swift to challenge you to combat and to violence far more inclusive than you think, are there by your election. Do not deny their presence nor their terrible results.[37]

These unrecognized beliefs necessitate our vigilance; we must be watchful for the "least decision to choose attack instead of love," recognize it as a "hidden warrior," and choose against it. In this stage we cooperate with the Holy Spirit as He sorts out our thoughts:

He sorts out the true from the false in your mind, and teaches you to judge every thought you allow to enter it in the light of what God put there. Whatever is in accord with this light He retains, to strengthen the Kingdom in you. What is partly in accord with it He accepts and purifies. But what is out of accord entirely He rejects by judging against.[38]

This stage is thus a period of watchful self-evaluation, a time in which we willingly bring our thoughts to the Holy Spirit for His help in judging them. If this sounds stressful, in fact it is not. Vigilance is against thoughts of attack and conflict, and freeing our minds of conflict brings only peace. The more watchful we are, the more peaceful we become.

We learn that, "While the first step seems to increase conflict and the second may still entail conflict to some extent, this step calls for constant vigilance against it."[39] In the first step the ego was strong in our minds, and the conflict with the ideas of love seemed great; in the second step, the balance was tilting away from the ego towards the Holy Spirit. Now, we are firmly aligned with Him, and are ever watchful for remnants of the ego thought system that still persist in our minds. If conflict arises, we do not despair, but take it as a warning signal; the conflict is exactly what we no longer want. Phase Two brings a relief from conflict precisely because we are watchful not to allow conflict to enter our minds.

We also watch against judgment within the mind, and let it go. Letting go of judgment brings an enormous release, and deep peace.[40]

The rich and expanding rewards motivate us to even more careful vigilance.

The third lesson goes beyond the divided state of the first two and moves towards integration, or single-mindedness.[41] We are guarding our mind and allowing in it only what God put there;[42] that is what it means to accept our mind as God created it. We are allowing God's thoughts in and keeping other thoughts out. We are protecting our minds and identifying only with the center, that is, with spirit.[43] This is the final preparation process for "the translation of *having* into *being*,"[44] or the shift into the real world.

Although filled with growing peace and joy, this is not yet a time of rest. We are told we must use effort.

> Vigilance does require effort, but only until you learn that effort itself is unnecessary. You have exerted great effort to preserve what you made because it was not true. Therefore, you must now turn your effort against it. Only this can cancel out the need for effort, and call upon the being which you both *have* and *are*. This recognition is wholly without effort since it is already true and needs no protection.[45]

This stage will continue until the mind is wholly unified in right-mindedness. Vigilance is the same evaluation process which is called "your part in the Atonement" at the end of Chapter 2 of the Text, where it is presented as the process of the Last Judgment, in which we separate the false from the true, and preserve only the good.[46]

One of the best summaries of what vigilance is like is given in Workbook Lesson 254:

> Let every voice but God's be still in me.
>
> Today we let no ego thoughts direct our words or actions. When such thoughts occur, we quietly step back and look at them, and then we let them go. We do not want what they would bring with them. And so we do not choose to keep them. They are silent now. And in the stillness, hallowed by His Love, God speaks to us and tells us of our will, as we have chosen to remember Him.[47]

Finding Our Function: Vigilance for the Kingdom

Phase Two emphasizes accepting the Atonement, which is the function of a miracle worker. At first it may seem that the emphasis of the Course on accepting the Atonement for ourselves means simply getting ourselves healed and ignoring the rest of the world, a rather self-centered approach to spirituality. Many students of the Course make this mistake. And it *is* a mistake. The Course is quick to point out that looking for the Holy Spirit in ourselves alone is a mistake because that is not where He is;[48] He is "the shared inspiration of the Sonship."[49] He belongs to no one of us alone; He belongs to all of us together. If He is "God's Answer to the separation,"[50] then hearing His Voice must bring us to an awareness of our oneness. Listening to His Voice "implies the decision to share It in order to hear It yourself."[51]

Accepting the Atonement means a desire to join rather than separate. I do not join with my brother's dreams of separation but I do join with *him*.[52] Accepting the Atonement is the sole responsibility of the miracle worker,[53] that is, one who brings miracles of healing to others. When you accept the Atonement, you have recognized for yourself "that mind is the only creative level, and that its errors are healed by the Atonement."[54] When that happens, something very basic shifts in your mind. You begin to bring healing to others. You start to work miracles.

> Once you accept this, your mind can only heal. By denying your mind any destructive potential and reinstating its purely constructive powers, you place yourself in a position to undo the level confusion of others. The message you then give to them is the truth that their minds are similarly constructive, and their miscreations cannot hurt them.[55]

In other words, when you are healed you discover that you are a healer by your very nature. In withdrawing your projections and accepting healing you have recognized that your own miscreations can't hurt you, and that your mind is "purely constructive." Your mind gives rather than gets; heals rather than attacks; accepts rather than rejects. You are healed by rediscovering the fact that you are a healer, and nothing less.

Phase Two is the stage in which we will accept our function as miracle workers and fulfill it. Miracles are intensely interpersonal,[56] and that means relationships. This stage is both one of accepting the Atonement for ourselves and becoming *part of* the Atonement through extending it to others.

> When you have been restored to the recognition of your original state, you naturally become part of the Atonement yourself. As you share my unwillingness to accept error in yourself and others [the essense of what we learn in Phase One], you must join the great crusade to correct it; listen to my voice, learn to undo error and act to correct it.[57]

Till now, perhaps, we thought the journey was for ourselves alone. That was only the "very preliminary" and "preliminary" steps. Now we realize that we cannot enter Heaven without the Sonship. "Never forget that the Sonship is your salvation, for the Sonship is your Self."[58] Salvation of the world depends on us; this function is what our willingness is really for.

> We are the joint will of the Sonship, whose Wholeness is for all. We begin the journey back by setting out together [you and Jesus], and gather in our brothers as we continue together.[59]

In *The Song of Prayer,* the "second level" of prayer is "Praying with Others."[60] At this level of prayer, which is parallel to Step Three of the journey, sharing begins. The key thought which brings entry to this level is that I and my brother are journeying together:

> The key to rising further still in prayer lies in this simple thought; this change of mind:
>
> *We go together, you and I.*[61]

At this level joining and sharing become integral parts of the journey. We experience a very specific change of mind from a focus on individual salvation to the awareness of an inescapable oneness, and we stop perceiving enemies and perceive our savior instead. The healing of others becomes our way home.

This change of mind is what moves us out of the preliminary phase and into the heart and soul of the journey. It *is* the transition from Phase

One to Two. "We go together, you and I." We are vigilant to hold the wholeness of the Sonship in our minds, refusing to allow doubt to enter.[62] We see that recognizing our brothers and sisters as whole, forgiven, and in the Kingdom is the way that we claim our own inheritance. In welcoming them we find our own welcome. The meaning of "To have, give all to all" begins to resonate within our being.

Workbook Lesson 166 reminds us that once we have decided to accept the gifts of God, there is one more thing we have to remember: the gifts are not for us alone.

> Yet He reminds you still of one thing more you had forgotten. For His touch on you has made you like Himself. The gifts you have are not for you alone. What He has come to offer you, you now must learn to give. This is the lesson that His giving holds, for He has saved you from the solitude you sought to make in which to hide from God....
>
> ...You are entrusted with the world's release from pain.[63]

The message is repeated over and over in the Course, in Workbook and Text alike:

> I call upon you to teach what you have learned, because by so doing you can depend on it.[64]

> By following Him you are led back to God where you belong, and how can you find the way except by taking your brother with you? My part in the Atonement is not complete until you join it and give it away. As you teach so shall you learn.[65]

We are here to help each other on the journey. If our brother makes mistakes, we can take them from him through our forgiveness: "His mistakes can cause delay, which it is given you to take from him, that both may end a journey that has never begun, and needs no end."[66]

We each are given a special function, certain persons we are specially suited to forgive.[67] What we have to share is our own healing, and those who can learn and be healed through us will be drawn to us, and we to them. The Course tells us that our function is our happiness.

There can be no greater joy in this world than finding our purpose and carrying it out. Healing others heals us, and brings a kind of happiness we cannot know otherwise.

Through holy relationships we learn our general function "of restoring [our] Father's laws to what was held outside them, and finding what was lost."[68] Those holy relationships become sources of healing to the entire world: "Two voices raised together call to the hearts of everyone, to let them beat as one."[69] The holy relationships are like laboratories where we practice and learn the forgiveness and love that we can then apply to the entire world.

Holy relationships have, in themselves, their own special function in bringing healing into the world. Our part in the plan is to cooperate with the Holy Spirit in transforming our unholy relationships into holy ones, and allowing Him to use them to heal the world. This is no easy process, but the Course calls this the "last undoing" and says it will bring us at last to know our true Self:

> Be not afraid to look upon the special hate relationship, for freedom lies in looking at it....For the special love relationship, in which the meaning of love is hidden, is undertaken solely to offset the hate, but not to let it go. Your salvation will rise clearly before your open eyes as you look on this....
>
> ...You will go through this last undoing quite unharmed, and will at last emerge as yourself. This is the last step in the readiness for God.[70]

The whole purpose of the journey is to end our separation from God and the universe of His creation. Why should it be surprising that we work this out in the context of specific relationships? How can we learn the larger lesson if we cannot learn the smaller one?

The Holy Spirit instructs us in our function using specific examples. We begin with the people closest to us. We don't have to go far to find His lessons:

> If He wills you to have it [salvation], He must have made it possible and easy to obtain it. Your brothers are everywhere. You do not have to seek far for salvation. Every minute and every second gives you a chance to save yourself.[71]

On our journey we are approaching God. How do we do so? God "is approached through the appreciation of His Son."[72] "Would *you* remember the Father? Accept His Son and you will remember Him."[73] Through the exercise of our function in forgiving and healing those around us, through appreciating them as the gifts of God to us, we approach God Himself. There is no other way.

> You who are beginning to wake are still aware of dreams, and have not yet forgotten them. The forgetting of dreams and the awareness of Christ come with the awakening of others to share your redemption.
>
> ...Redemption is recognized only by sharing it.[74]

Healing our relationships is "the last step in the readiness for God."[75] Steps One and Two were only preparation for this. We have travelled through the heart of darkness only to become the light of the world. Wholeness lives only in this—in recognizing that every living thing is sacred because God created it, and that we are sacred only if everyone is. Without everything, we are nothing. With Jesus, we say:

> My task is not completed until I have lifted every voice with mine.[76]

Our holy relationships in this world are meant to be constant reminders of the holy instants we spend with God. Holy instants alone are not enough.

> Without expression [the holy instant] is not remembered. The holy relationship is a constant reminder of the experience in which the relationship became what it is.[77]

We need one another to hold the experience of the holy instant in our awareness. In our acceptance of our brother, and in our thanks and gratitude for his gifts to us, we are sharing and expressing the holy instant, and thus retaining our awareness of it. If we fail in this, we lose the effectiveness of the holy instant in our lives.[78]

Together, the partners in a holy relationship have a sacred and high calling, a special function in God's plan. The healing of one relationship becomes the healing of the entire world as what is within us extends and covers the world in its blessing of inclusion. The Holy Spirit does the work of extension through us, leading us in what appears to be busy activity, but is actually effortless as we give ourselves to be His instruments in the world.

> You have been called, together with your brother, to the most holy function this world contains. It is the only one that has no limits, and reaches out to every broken fragment of the Sonship with healing and uniting comfort. This is offered you, in your holy relationship....The holy light that brought you and him together must extend, as you accepted it.[79]

The pattern seems to be that, having accepted a single purpose and becoming of one mind with the Holy Spirit, we find ourselves joining in relationship with others who come to share the same purpose with us. Not all our partners will overtly share our purpose; there may be open opposition. Some, however, join with us in common purpose. Together, each healed relationship will find its function. Carrying out that function of extension and healing is the final step in bringing us to the real world.

> Each holy relationship must enter here, to learn its special function in the Holy Spirit's plan, now that it shares His purpose. And as this purpose is fulfilled, a new world rises in which sin can enter not.[80]

Once we have accepted the Holy Spirit's plan for ourselves as our only purpose, finding and filling our function in relationships, the Holy Spirit takes care of everything else for us:

> Once you accept His plan as the one function that you would fulfill, there will be nothing else the Holy Spirit will not arrange for you without your effort. He will go before you making straight your path, and leaving in your way no stones to trip on, and no obstacles to bar your way. Nothing you need will be denied you.[81]

The final stretch of the journey becomes a straight path. Our only effort is to maintain our willing, single-minded cooperation with Him as He leads us onward. Everything else simply falls into place. We live for one thing only: to forgive, to free our brothers as Christ has freed us. "Here is the only purpose that gives this world, and the long journey through this world, whatever meaning lies in them."[82]

And this is how the journey ends for us. As we are vigilant, both for God (and against the ego) and for His Kingdom (the Sonship), our perception becomes more and more purified and aligned with the knowledge of Heaven. We accept our function as the light of the world. We see the world as having no purpose other than the healing of God's Son, the unification of every broken fragment of the Sonship in one healing brightness, and we devote our lives to that single function. When our forgiveness is complete with nothing and no one excluded, when every dark thought has at last been exposed to the light and released, we enter the real world, hearing only the Voice for God. We find perfect happiness in the perfect fulfillment of our only function; we are happy because we have a purpose and fulfill it. We are happy to be here, although we no longer believe that "here" really exists, because our task is not complete until every mind is healed. We wait only for God to take the last step:

> Together we will disappear into the Presence beyond the veil, not to be lost but found; not to be seen but known. And knowing, nothing in the plan God has established for salvation will be left undone. This is the journey's purpose, without which is the journey meaningless. Here is the peace of God, given to you eternally by Him. Here is the rest and quiet that you seek, the reason for the journey from the beginning.[83]

> When you perceive yourself without deceit, you will accept the real world in place of the false one you have made. And then your Father will lean down to you and take the last step for you, raising you unto Himself.[84]

---

[1] S-1.IV.2:2
[2] M-19.2:6-7
[3] T-1.IV.1:1-5
[4] M-4.I(A).6:1
[5] M-4.I(A).6:2
[6] M-4.I(A).6:3-8
[7] T-6.V(C).1:10-11
[8] M-4.I(A).6:9
[9] M-4.I(A).6:10
[10] M-4.I(A).7:3

[11] T-6.V(C).10:1
[12] T-23.I.1:1-2
[13] T-23.I.7:7
[14] T-24.In.1:1-2
[15] M-4.I(A).6:11-13
[16] T-20.IV.6:5
[17] T-20.IV.7:3
[18] T-11.I.1:3
[19] T-6.V(C).2:8
[20] M- 4.I(A).7:1

[21] T-30.V.8:1-2
[22] M-4.I(A).7:7-9
[23] S-1.IV.2:2
[24] M-10.3:1
[25] T-24.VI.7:2
[26] T-2.VII.1:7-9
[27] M-4.VIII.1:1
[28] T-14.III.3:2
[29] M-22.2:2
[30] M-22.2:4-9, boldface added
[31] T-6.V(C).3:1-5
[32] Random House Dictionary
[33] T-13.VII.2:2
[34] T-6.V(C).3:2
[35] T-6.V(C).4:5
[36] Random House Dictionary
[37] T-24.I.2:2, 4, 6-7
[38] T-6.V(C).1:2-5
[39] T-6.V(C).4:1
[40] T-3.VI.3:1
[41] T-6.V(C).5:3
[42] T-6.V(C).5:4
[43] T-6.V(C).7:1
[44] T-6.V(C).5:8
[45] T-6.V(C).10:4-8
[46] T-2.VIII.5:11, 4:1, 4:3
[47] W-pII.254.Heading, 2
[48] T-5.III.4:1-5
[49] T-5.I.7:1
[50] T-5.II.2:5
[51] T-5.IV.4:2
[52] T-28.IV.1:1, 2, 6, 2:5-7, 10:1

[53] T-2.V.5:1
[54] T-2.V.5:2
[55] T-2.V.5:3-5
[56] T-1.II.1:4
[57] T-1.III.1:5-6
[58] T-11.IV.1:1
[59] T-8.VI.1:1-2
[60] S-1.IV.Heading
[61] S-1.IV.1:7-8
[62] T-6.V(C).8:2
[63] W-pI.166.12:1-5, 14:6
[64] T-5.IV.5:4
[65] T-5.IV.6:2-4
[66] T-24.VI.8:3
[67] T-25.VI.4:2-3 and T-26.II.6:5-6
[68] T-20.V.1:3
[69] T-20.V.2:3
[70] T-16.IV.1:1, 3-4, 2:3-4
[71] T-9.VII.1:3-6
[72] T-11.IV.7:2
[73] T-11.V.17:1
[74] T-11.VI.8:7-8, 9:6
[75] T-16.IV.2:4
[76] T-13.VII.17:2
[77] T-17.V.1:5-6
[78] T-17.V.11:10
[79] T-18.I.13:1-3, 6
[80] T-20.IV.6:6-7
[81] T-20.IV.8:4-6
[82] T-19.IV(D).21:4
[83] T-19.IV(D).19:1-5
[84] T-11.VIII.15:4-5

Chapter 7

Being a Happy Learner

The map of the journey is as complete as we can make it in the brief span of this book. Innumerable details have been left out. To find out what they are, however, you need only read *A Course in Miracles* itself, because providing those details is the purpose of its 1249 pages. As we look now at the complete map, we need to remember that all of it is an illusion to correct our initial illusion of separation. We need to remember also that any such division into steps is not absolute; we may experience some overlap, some aspects of the later steps at the beginning, or of the early steps even toward the end.

The purpose of this closing chapter is simply to encourage you, and myself, to determine to complete this journey with as little delay as possible. As we travel we can travel with joy; as we learn, we can be happy learners. Nothing speeds us on our journey like happy acceptance of the journey; nothing slows us down like discontent with its progress.

Not a Rosy Picture

We must be realistic about the journey. Its overall picture could never be described as "rosy." In fact it seems in many respects rather dark and somber. Of the six periods mentioned in "Development of Trust," four do not sound particularly happy—"undoing," "sorting out," "relinquishment," and "unsettling"—although the "unsettling" period is also a time of steadily increasing joy as we carry out our part in the Holy Spirit's plan. Since the final period, "achievement," is in fact the end of the journey, there is actually only one period in the journey that has a wholly positive designation, the "period of rest," and even that rest is short-lived, no more than a rest stop along the highway to God.

I can think of no bigger mistake than to imagine that the spiritual path of the Course is nothing but joy and happiness, blue skies, and paths strewn with rose petals. Pain is not necessary for our journey. Not necessary, but rarely wholly avoided. Very few of us recognize right from the start that all pain comes from our own resistance to healing, from our own attempts to constrict the flow of God's Love through us. That is the whole point of Phase One, and until we learn that we are the ones causing our own pain, we cannot enter the happier path of Phase Two.

We are tempted to want to skip Phase One and go directly to "the quicker ascent," but that is simply impossible. Phase Two cannot occur without Phase One. As Ken Wapnick so often points out, we cannot skip steps. We have to pass through undoing, sorting out, and relinquishing before we can find rest. The rest is provided only to allow us to gather strength, as well as companions, for the rest of the journey.

We cannot avoid the process of unmasking our egos, no matter how much we want to avoid the fear and conflict entailed in that process. Indeed, this journey seems to be one "through fear to love."[1] "We have repeatedly emphasized the need to recognize fear and face it without disguise as a crucial step in the undoing of the ego."[2] The enemy we fear is a toothless tiger, but until we face it we will not know that, and will remain cowering in our fear.

> Take off the covers and look at what you are afraid of. Only the anticipation will frighten you, for the reality of nothingness cannot be frightening.[3]

If you get one thing from this consideration of the spiritual journey, I hope it is this: there is more to this than I thought. The Course is a very serious, very complete, and very thorough course of spiritual development.

Allen Watson

No Quick and Easy Fix

The Course does not promise enlightenment in a weekend. Salvation is not going to be handed to you on a silver platter. Like it or not, this is going to take time. Looking at the journey shows us this. Two of the steps mention lengths of time. In the first lesson of the Holy Spirit we are told that "some remain at this step for a long time, experiencing very acute conflict."[4] The fifth period in the development of trust, much later in the journey, tells us, "Now he must attain a state that may remain impossible to reach for a long, long time."[5] The Course is not promising a quick and easy fix.

Yes, it is true that the Course tells us enlightenment is but a recognition[6]—but what a recognition! The Atonement is already accomplished and all we need to do is recognize it, all we need to do is to stop denying it. That *could* happen in any instant, it is true.

Yet the thing preventing that recognition, the thing which blocks the awareness of love's presence, is very firmly set in place. Our ego is no small thing; it has been manufactured by our minds, with all the power given our minds by God. If we underestimate the power of our ego, we are underestimating the power of our own mind which manufactured it, and in so doing we are underestimating the very thing that is our way out of hell. The ego is not so easily dismissed. "No one dismisses something he considers part of himself."[7] Helping us to realize how much of our thinking is ego-directed is one clear purpose of the Course.[8]

> The ego has no power to distract you unless you give
> it the power to do so. The ego's voice is an hallucination.
> You cannot expect it to say "I am not real."[9]

The ego won't walk up to you and identify itself. It has spent millenia learning how to hide itself from you, and it will take effort on your part to expose it. Illusions are based on clever deception; they are not obvious. The ego is exceedingly devious and hides beneath multiple layers of camouflage. This is why transcending it is not as easy as many people think.

You have to catch it in the act. The ego is an activity of your mind; it is something you are "doing." If you do not realize you are doing it, you won't stop. You won't *know* to stop. "All" you have to do is to stop doing it; simply recognize what you have been doing and stop. But that is no small task.

Your active involvement is necessary to dispel the ego. "You may also think that it would be easy enough for the Holy Spirit to show it to you, and to dispel it without the need for you to raise it to awareness yourself."[10] We may think that, but obviously Jesus is saying it is not so: we cannot dispel the ego without raising it to awareness ourselves. We have to raise it to awareness because we are the ones hiding it. Jesus will not violate our will and do it for us. We must raise it to awareness so that the Holy Spirit can dispel it. This is why the journey can take so long.

> But what you hide He [the Holy Spirit] cannot look upon. He sees for you, and unless you look with Him He cannot see. The vision of Christ is not for Him alone, but for Him with you.[11]

"Yet you are not asked to dispel your hallucinations alone."[12] You must cooperate, certainly. You must look at your ego and uncover its machinations, but you are not asked to try to dispel it by yourself.

> If you will look, the Holy Spirit will judge, and He will judge truly. Yet He cannot shine away what you keep hidden, for you have not offered it to Him and He cannot take it from you.[13]

You must expose the hidden ego; the Holy Spirit shines it away. When you uncover your ego you bring it to Him, and He looks past it to the Atonement. He dismisses the ego for you.

> When you unite with me you are uniting without the ego, because I have renounced the ego in myself and therefore cannot unite with yours. Our union is therefore the way to renounce the ego in you. The truth in both of us is beyond the ego. Our success in transcending the ego is guaranteed by God.[14]

Our Destination: The Real World

Many times in the Course Jesus stops and paints a picture for us of what the real world is like. I am certain that one of his reasons is to encourage us to move on and to move quickly. He knows that the way is not always easy, and the task sometimes appears greater than we can handle. He knows because he has already travelled this road. So he reminds us again of where we are going, enticing us to lift up our heads and keep walking towards home.

> Yet the real world has the power to touch you even here, because you love it. And what you call with love will come to you. Love always answers, being unable to deny a call for help, or not to hear the cries of pain that rise to it from every part of this strange world you made but do not want.[15]

"Love always answers." We can rest assured of that. We *will* reach the real world, though it may seem intolerably distant at times. It is not distant. It is near. It is here. It is now, always within our grasp. The holy instant shows us this; at any time, in any place, we can catch a glimpse of that real world, breathe its air, experience its peace, and marvel at its beauty.

> In no fantasy have you ever seen anything so lovely. Nothing you see here, sleeping or waking, comes near to such loveliness. And nothing will you value like unto this, nor hold so dear. Nothing that you remember that made your heart sing with joy has ever brought you even a little part of the happiness this sight will bring you. For you will see the Son of God. You will behold the beauty the Holy Spirit loves to look upon, and which He thanks the Father for. He was created to see this for you, until you learned to see it for yourself. And all His teaching leads to seeing it and giving thanks with Him.

> This loveliness is not a fantasy. It is the real world, bright and clean and new, with everything sparkling under the open sun....This little step, so small it has escaped your notice, is a stride through time into eternity, beyond all ugliness into beauty that will enchant you, and will never cease to cause you wonderment at its perfection.[16]

Over and over the Course reminds us that this *is* what we want. It fills the unvoiced longing of every heart. The real world contains "the forgotten song"[17] that we dimly retain in memory and long for.

Look back no longer, for what lies ahead is all you ever wanted in your heart. Give up the world! But not to sacrifice. You never wanted it.[18]

Following with Joy

The Holy Spirit is leading us to Christ and to the real world. Where else might we want to go? What other need have we but to awake in Christ?

> Then follow Him in joy, with faith that He will lead you safely through all dangers to your peace of mind this world may set before you. Kneel not before the altars to sacrifice, and seek not what you will surely lose. Content yourself with what you will as surely keep, and be not restless, for you undertake a quiet journey to the peace of God, where He would have you be in quietness.[19]

The world will throw a lot of "dangers to your peace of mind" at you. The Holy Spirit can lead you safely through all of them, if you will follow Him in joy. We may be tempted to see the journey as hard and to view what we are being called upon to do as a sacrifice, but Jesus asks us not to kneel at that altar, nor to stop to long after things in this world that inevitably must be lost in the end. What we are seeking is something that cannot be lost, not ever, and surely that is enough.

"Be not restless," he counsels us. How incongruous it is for us to be restless on a journey to peace! The restlessness is only another manifestation of the problem we are journeying to leave. It is restlessness that we are leaving behind. He asks us to be patient, knowing that infinite patience has immediate results; knowing that we can afford to be patient if we are certain of the outcome. He asks us to be content with healing, and not to be discontent with the fact that we are not instantly healed. He tells us to be happy learners:

> The Holy Spirit needs a happy learner, in whom His mission can be happily accomplished.[20]

> The happy learner cannot feel guilty about learning. This is so essential to learning that it should never be forgotten.[21]

Learning is living here, as creating is being in Heaven.[22]

In other words, learning is what life is for. So let's stop griping about the lessons and just learn them. Let's stop feeling guilty because we still have lessons to learn. Letting go of the guilt of being "not there yet" is *essential* to learning, because "guilt is interference, not salvation."[23] Guilt interferes with the learning process. There is no such thing as a "guilty learner" because guilt keeps us from learning anything. Of course it does, because what we are being taught is that God's Son is guiltless. Feeling guilty about our "lack" of spiritual growth is really just another way we have of avoiding the next step in the journey.

Our Elder Brother Goes with Us

Jesus becomes our constant companion on the road we travel. He makes several promises to support us personally in our journey.

> I go before you because I am beyond the ego. Reach, therefore, for my hand because you want to transcend the ego. My strength will never be wanting, and if you choose to share it you will do so. I give it willingly and gladly, because I need you as much as you need me.[24]

If you want to travel safely, reach for the hand of Jesus. He knows the way; he has travelled the road before. He will make up for what you lack until you know you do not lack it. He shares his strength with you willingly and gladly *because* he knows the truth: He needs you as much as you need him. You are a part of him he cannot leave behind.

> My brother, you are part of God and part of me. When you have at last looked at the ego's foundation without shrinking you will also have looked upon ours. I come to you from our Father to offer you everything again. Do not refuse it in order to keep a dark cornerstone hidden, for its protection will not save you. I give you the lamp and I will go with you. You will not take this journey alone. I will lead you to your true Father, Who hath need of you, as I have. Will you not answer the call of love with joy?[25]

You will not take this journey alone; Jesus goes with you, and leads you to our Father. You need that help in the dark and twisted passages we travel through. We all need it. As tempting as it may seem to keep the repugnant ego hidden, only when we look at it "without shrinking" can it be dispelled forever. Our greatest help in looking at the ego's foundation without fear is the presence of one who looks with us through the gentle eyes of forgiveness. If he is with us we can look at anything.

> Our Love awaits us as we go to Him, and walks beside us showing us the way. He fails in nothing. He is the End we seek, and He the Means by which we go to Him.[26]

> The sight of Christ is all there is to see. The song of Christ is all there is to hear. The hand of Christ is all there is to hold. There is no journey but to walk with him.[27]

Look Forward

> Look forward, then; in confidence walk with a happy heart that beats in hope and does not pound in fear.[28]

We can go on. This journey is possible. No, not simply possible— inevitable. It is a journey without distance and we cannot fail to complete it. It is inevitable because its goal is the truth. "You travel but in dreams, while safe at home."[29]

> Today in gratitude we lift our hearts above despair, and raise our thankful eyes, no longer looking downward to the dust. We sing the song of thankfulness today, in honor of the Self that God has willed to be our true Identity in Him. Today we smile on everyone we see, and walk with lightened footsteps as we go to do what is appointed us to do.[30]

Whenever I consider the spiritual journey I am encouraged to lift my heart and walk with lightened footsteps. It is a marvellous journey, and worthy of our every effort, deserving of all our confidence. Let us join, then, in these final thoughts from Review V in the Workbook:

> Our footsteps have not been unwavering, and doubts have made us walk uncertainly and slowly on the road this course sets forth. But now we hasten on, for we approach a greater certainty, a firmer purpose and a surer goal.

> Steady our feet, our Father....Lead our practicing as does a father lead a little child along a way he does not understand....

...And if we stumble, You will raise us up. If we forget the way, we count upon Your sure remembering. We wander off, but You will not forget to call us back. Quicken our footsteps now, that we may walk more certainly and quickly unto You.[31]

---

[1] T-16.IV.11:1
[2] T-12.I.8:5
[3] T-12.II.5:2-3
[4] T-6.V(A).6:6
[5] M-4.I(A).7:7
[6] W.pI.188.1:4
[7] T-4:II.4:3
[8] T-4.VI.1:4
[9] T-8.I.2:1-3
[10] T-13.III.1:2
[11] T-14.VII.6:5-7
[12] T-8.I.2:4
[13] T-12.II.9:7-8
[14] T-8.V.4:1-4
[15] T-13.VII.4:1-3
[16] T-17.II.1:2-2:2, 6

[17] T-21.I.6-7
[18] T-30.V.9:3-6
[19] T-13.VII.15:1-3
[20] T-14.II.1:1
[21] T-14.III.1:1-2
[22] T-14.III.3:2
[23] T-14.III.1:4
[24] T-8.V.6:7-10
[25] T-11.In.4
[26] W-pII.302.2:1-3
[27] T-24.V.7:7-10
[28] T-30.V.10:8
[29] T-13.VII.17:7
[30] W-pI.123.4
[31] W-rV.In.1:5-6, 2:1, 5, 3:2-5

The Circle's Mission Statement

To discern the author's vision of *A Course in Miracles* and manifest that in our lives, in the lives of students, and in the world.

1 To faithfully discern the author's vision of *A Course in Miracles*.

In interpreting the Course we strive for total fidelity to its words and the meanings they express. We thereby seek to discover the Course as the author saw it.

2 To be an instrument in Jesus' plan to manifest his vision of the Course in the lives of students and in the world.

We consider this to be Jesus' organization and therefore we attempt to follow his guidance in all we do. Our goal is to help students understand, as well as discern for themselves, the Course's thought system as he intended, and use it as he meant it to be used—as a literal program in spiritual awakening. Through doing so we hope to help ground in the world the intended way of doing the Course, here at the beginning of its history.

3 To help spark an enduring tradition based entirely on students joining together in doing the Course as the author envisioned.

We have a vision of local Course support systems composed of teachers, students, healers, and groups, all there to support one another in making full use of the Course. These support systems, as they continue and multiply, will together comprise an enduring spiritual tradition, dedicated solely to doing the Course as the author intended. Our goal is to help spark this tradition, and to assist others in doing the same.

4 To become an embodiment, a birthplace of this enduring spiritual tradition.

To help spark this tradition we must first become a model for it ourselves. This requires that we at the Circle follow the Course as our individual path; that we ourselves learn forgiveness through its program. It requires that we join with each other in a group holy relationship dedicated to the common goal of awakening through the Course. It also requires that we cultivate a local support system here in Sedona, and that we have a facility where others could join with us in learning this approach to the Course. Through all of this we hope to become a seed for an ongoing spiritual tradition based on *A Course in Miracles*.

Books & Booklets in This Series

Commentaries on *A Course in Miracles*
by Robert Perry and Allen Watson

1. **Seeing the Face of Christ in All Our Brothers** *by Perry*. How we can see the Presence of God in others. $5.00

3. **Shrouded Vaults of the Mind** *by Perry*. Draws a map of the mind based on the Course, and takes you on a tour through its many levels. $5.00

4. **Guidance: Living the Inspired Life** *by Perry*. Sketches an overall perspective on guidance and its place on the spiritual path. $7.00

8. **A Healed Mind Does Not Plan** *by Watson*. Examines our approach to planning and decision-making, showing how it is possible to leave the direction of our lives up to the Holy Spirit. $5.00

9. **Through Fear to Love** *by Watson*. Explores two sections from the Course that deal with our fear of redemption. Leads the reader to see how it is possible to look upon ourselves with love. $5.00

10. **The Journey Home** *by Watson*. Presents a description of our spiritual destination and what we must go through to get there. $8.50

11. **Everything You Always Wanted to Know About Judgment but Were Too Busy Doing It to Notice** *by Perry and Watson*. A survey of various teachings about judgment in the Course. $8.00

12. **The Certainty of Salvation** *by Perry and Watson*. How we can become certain that we will find our way to God. $5.00

13. **What Is Death?** *by Watson*. The Course's view of what death really is. $5.00

14. **The Workbook as a Spiritual Practice** *by Perry*. A guide for getting the most out of the Workbook. $5.00

15. **I Need Do Nothing: Finding the Quiet Center** *by Watson*. An in-depth discussion of one of the most misunderstood sections of the Course. $5.00

16. **A Course Glossary** *by Perry*. 150 definitions of terms and phrases from the Course, for students and study groups. $7.00

17. Seeing the Bible Differently: How *A Course in Miracles* Views the Bible *by Watson.* Shows the similarities, differences, and continuity between the Course and the Bible. $6.00

18. Relationships as a Spiritual Journey: From Specialness to Holiness *by Perry.* Describes the Course's unique view of how we can find God through the transformation of our relationships. $11.00

19. A Workbook Companion Volume I *by Watson and Perry.* Commentaries on Lessons 1 - 120. $16.00

20. A Workbook Companion Volume II *by Watson and Perry.* Commentaries on Lessons 121 - 243. $16.00

21. A Workbook Companion Volume III *by Watson and Perry.* Commentaries on Lessons 244 - 365. $18.00

22. The Answer Is a Miracle *by Perry and Watson.* Looks at what the Course means by miracles, and how we can experience them in our lives. $7.00

23. Let Me Remember You *by Perry and Watson.* Regaining a sense of God's relevance, both in the Course and in our lives. $10.00

24. Bringing the Course to Life: How to Unlock the Meaning of *A Course in Miracles* for Yourself *by Watson and Perry.* Designed to teach the student, through instruction, example and exercises, how to read the Course so that the experience becomes a personal encounter with the truth. $12.00

25. Reality and Illusion: An Overview of Course Metaphysics *by Perry.* Examines the Course's lofty vision of reality, its account of the events which gave birth to our current existence, and how the Course views the relationship between ultimate reality and the illusory world of separation. $11.00

For shipping rates, a complete catalog of our products and services, or for information about events, please contact us at:

The Circle of Atonement
Teaching and Healing Center
P.O. Box 4238
W. Sedona, AZ 86340
(928) 282-0790 Fax: (928) 282-0523
E-mail: info@circleofa.com
Website: www.circleofa.com